BORN TO FIGHT

BORN TO FIGHT

Richy Horsley with Stephen Richards

JOHN BLAKE

Published by John Blake Publishing Ltd,
3 Bramber Court, 2 Bramber Road,
London W14 9PB, England

www.blake.co.uk

First published in paperback in 2008

ISBN: 978 1 84454 556 8

British Library Cataloguing-in-Publication Data:

A catalogue record for this book is available from the British Library.

Design by www.envydesign.co.uk

Printed in Great Britain by CPI Bookmarque, Croydon CRO 4TD

1 3 5 7 9 10 8 6 4 2

Papers used by John Blake Publishing are natural, recyclable products
made from wood grown in sustainable forests. The manufacturing
processes conform to the environmental regulations of the country of
origin.

Every attempt has been made to contact the relevant copyright-holders,
but some were unobtainable. We would be grateful if the appropriate
people could contact us.

For my father, Tom 'Blood' Horsley and my mother, Brenda

CONTENTS

FOREWORD

How can you sum up Richy Horsley in just a few words? He's a legend in the fight game, and deservedly so. His heart is as big as he is and that's pretty fucking big, as it happens.

What separates him from other hard men is the fact that he's got a brain and a good one at that, as this book will show you. It's a cut above the others on the hard-men shelf in the bookshop and I certainly thought it was compelling reading – and a very good film it would make as well. I can't think who would play Richy Horsley but Richy himself, and as cocky flash bastards go, he's as good as you get and that's coming from the cockiest, flashiest bastard of them all, ME. Love you to bits, Richy

Dave Courtney OBE

TRIBUTES TO RICHY 'CRAZY HORSE' HORSLEY

Kevin 'Bulldog' Bennett – Commonwealth
Lightweight Champion

I came to Hartlepool in October 1998, having recently left the armed forces. Richy was one of the first people I met. Although I had just arrived, I had already heard of the man who was spoken of as a legend. We spoke less than three sentences on that first meeting and I was still left wondering what type of person he was.

However, as time went on and I got to know the man they call Crazy Horse, I found him to be a very personal man who chose his words carefully and never let his mouth run away. He is a generous man in his thoughts and feelings to others and always had the ability to turn the most serious of situations into a laugh. A man that's not always understood by outsiders, Richy is also a gentle giant with a sense of humour that makes people crave his company. It's a pleasure, and an honour, to call him a friend.

Charles Bronson – Britain's Most Dangerous Prisoner

Some men are just born to fight, it's in their blood. They can't do anything about it, they have to fight. A fighter isn't necessarily a psycho or a thug, far from it. Most fighters are gentlemen, men of pride, men of honour. Put a baby in their arms and they cry with joy like any man. But if you fuck with a fighter you've got to expect the consequences. You're gonna get hurt, you may even die. No man is invincible. Even fighters at times feel defeat ... some even die! But bet your arse on it, if they don't die, they're coming back for more. Richy Horsley is one of these special breeds of men and I'm honoured to know the man. Max Respect.

Terry Currie – Promoter of Unlicensed Boxing

Richy Horsley is a true fighter, the type of lionhearted fighting man that is becoming harder to find. When I asked Richy to fight on my unlicensed promotion, he was reluctant at first but, like all true warriors, he couldn't resist a challenge for long; fighters pride won the day and he finally agreed and got straight into training.

On the night of the fight, he was the true focused professional and performed a calm clinical demolition job inside one round ... HE WAS BACK.

Julian Davies – Author of *Street Fighters* and Former Heavyweight Boxer

I once wrote a book on fighters and was given Richy's name as a fighter that should be in the book. He wasn't hard to find because so many people up North knew him or had heard of him. After meeting Richy, I realised that without him the book would never have been finished. That was a few years ago and I still get e-mails from all around the world asking after Richy.

His story touched so many readers that they seem to feel compelled to seek out further information on this great man. Richy is a giant of a man with a big heart; his story has inspired me and others like myself. I'm proud to regard myself as one of his friends.

John Dawson – Founder of Conceptional Combat Science, 5th Dan Master at Budo, 4th Dan Tae Kwon Do, 4th Dan Karpa Thai Boxing, British and European Individual and Team Champion, and Author of *Ever Perpetual Circles*

The personification of the fighting sciences and the fighting warrior are, to me, a way of life. Trial and error in combat is the deadliest of progressive scientific tests that best knows the pain of the battle-blemished body and wears upon the will. The spirit and cunning beckon for a total victory. I like Richy Horsley; he's a good man. We've trained on and off for almost 16 years, as I recall. This book publication is unique. It took me back to a time of nostalgia, a place where we both grew up. Characters and events of some I was privy to and others I heard about on the jungle telegraph, but one thing for sure is they were real. As a footnote all I can say is enjoy reading the trials and tribulations of this fighting warrior's victory spangled past ... you won't be disappointed.

Ian 'The Machine' Freeman – World Champion No Holds Barred Fighter

I'm from the same part of England as Richy, the North East. This part of the country has always had an unbelievable amount of very hard men. We breed them tough up here. Richy has had a good fighting name for years, whether it's with the use of boxing gloves or bare knuckles. The guy has a very big heart and a tremendous chin. He is a very loyal person who, if never crossed, is a friend for life. Good luck with the book, Richy, it's certain to be a winner.

Steve Holdsworth – Eurosport Boxing Commentator

Richy has all the ways and values of REAL hard men. He is a true gentleman outside the ropes and off the cobbles, doesn't go throwing his weight about or mouthing off, is never fazed if the odds are stacked against him and he detests bullies! These are the hallmarks of real warriors.

As I say, big-mouthed bullies are replacing these qualities. I am sure Richy won't mind me saying he is of the old school in his ways.

I would strongly encourage people to read this book. Not just for violence sake, but for inspiration in overcoming the odds. This book is genuine, some books are not!

The thing with Richy is, he is still doing it and anyone can go and witness him in action; the proof of him being a fighter is available to all. He doesn't make far-fetched claims or beef up his exploits with fantasy. This is a proper man and a proper warrior.

Richy Horsley, a feared fighting man? The man I met

was far from the man I had expected to meet. His reputation went before him but I found him to be charming. Like most people, if you stay on the right side, they are great. I'd hate to see anyone upset him though, as the rumours I had heard about his fighting prowess were alarming. Richy Horsley, a fighting man and a pussycat at the same time. Show respect to those hidden claws.

Harry Marsden – Boxing Trainer and Former Member of the Real Geordie Mafia

I've been in boxing most of my life and I've heard many things about this man, about his bravery, his fear for nothing or no one. I've heard so many stories about Richy and I always said to friends and myself that one day I'll meet this guy and, sure enough, I did.

Believe you me, what I'd heard was only a part of this man. I watched Richy fight down in London and a true warrior he was. I'm not easily impressed but I thought to myself, this is a guy I don't want as an enemy and, believe me, I've been around. Then I got to meet Richy and we got on great, swapped many stories, a real true gent as well as a real live warrior. I wish he'd been in my gym.

Now this man is wanting to take on my very close and dear friend Charles Bronson in Charlie's first fight when he's eventually released from prison – this will be a fight that will live on and on. I would love to train Richy for this fight but I can't, as I'll be taking care of Charlie. Both Charlie and myself look on Richy as someone who will never be forgotten in a real head-to-head whether in the ring or out. He is a man I'll always respect and admire, and

I'm glad to know I'm a friend of his. A real true warrior if ever there was one. Respect, Richy.

Jamie O'Keefe – Self-Protection Educator and Publisher

Richy Horsley: a man, a chancer, a trier, a father, a role model, a mate ... Yes, he's all of these and more. Richy is one of the good guys and living proof that good comes from bad if you search hard enough. Also of how one person is making changes to put right his far-removed darker side.

So why would a self-protection educator from the East End be writing a testimonial on a guy from Hartlepool? It's for no reason other than that feeling of life being a little unbalanced and Richy having not being given some of life's rewards and opportunities. His life was destined to be that of an underprivileged child who learned to love and protect those that loved him. The place in which he grew up could have been anywhere on this planet but just happened to be Hartlepool. Although by default this meant that he did not have as many opportunities to achieve as some in other areas of life have, he found opportunity within the clenched fist. Like most newly found and acquired abilities, this had to be fine tuned, as opposed to just being used in its raw state to hurt and punish just because he 'could'.

He did not always get it right and made more than his fair share of mistakes, but kept coming back for more until he started to get it right. Richy knew there was a 'good Richy' fighting to get out and to this day he is living proof of this.

One of the things I admire about him is that he actually 'walks the walk' in training as he lives.

I do not give out respect very often because it has become a lip-service comment on a par with the kind of thing banded about falsely at funerals. However, those I truly have respect and admiration for could be counted on one hand. Richy is one of those people for just being Richy. This man deserves a break and I hope this book is the first step towards this.

Roy 'Pretty Boy' Shaw – Former Bare-Knuckle Fighter and Unlicensed Boxing Champ

I saw Richy Horsley fight in London. He possesses the true warrior qualities that are getting rarer and rarer – guts, grit, heart and prepared to go into the trenches. A true modern-day gladiator.

Anthony Thomas – Former Heavyweight Boxer and Webmaster of the Official Lenny McLean Website

I first met Richy when I was helping my friend with the research for his first book, *Street Fighters*. The moment I met him, I knew Richy was a man of power and a true hard man. With the running of the Lenny McLean website and the various trips around the country looking for people for the *Street Fighters* book, I have met a lot of hard, tough men but, out of all these men, Richy stands out at the top; he is a true warrior and an unbelievable Street Fighter.

Steve Wraith – Former aide-de-camp to the Krays

Having met some of the top fighters and hard men over

the years in my capacity as the Kray brothers' business adviser, I feel that I am a good judge of character in the murky world of gangsters and fighters. Richy Horsley makes an immediate impression on you! He is a giant of a man, very much in the same mould as the late, great Lenny McLean. He fills a room on entry.

Once you make his acquaintance and shake his shovel-like hand, you realise that you are meeting a legend. Richy has established himself against all the odds as a top street fighter in the North East of England. In my line of work, word travels fast when you hear that someone in your neck of the woods can handle himself or is good with his fists. You tend to keep that name in the back of your mind in case you ever need to know it.

When I first met Richy, I was watching him fight at an unlicensed show in my second home ... London. I met up and talked to a lot of his supporters and everyone had a story to tell about the great man. Richy won the fight without breaking into a sweat with a knockout inside one minute. Awesome! I followed him and his entourage back to the dressing room and introduced myself. My hand was engulfed in a vicelike grip. We talked about the fight, home life, and people we both knew. A friendship had begun.

Since that day, I have followed Richy's career with a great deal of interest. Richy has now decided to, finally, put pen to paper and publish his story and let us walk around his memoirs. I for one can't wait to take a good look inside the mind of one of Britain's most respected gladiators.

Michael Hunter, Undefeated British Super Bantamweight Champion

Richy has been a friend of mine for a number of years. He's worked in my corner as an amateur and a professional and we've had some good times. Once you get to know him, he's a nice bloke. I've also seen him knock some big men out in street fights. Richy wasn't a bad heavyweight boxer either, he was very tough and as game as they come. I have nothing but the greatest respect for him. Good luck mate.

Jan Lamb, The Angel of the Underworld

Richy Horsley is a good and trusted friend. I am very glad to see he has now written his autobiography. I am certain this book is going to be a very big seller. Richy has had a very interesting life and is well liked and respected by lots of people. I am very proud to write a little tribute. RESPECT.

INTRODUCTION

To the unsuspecting, Richy Horsley could be just any old unassuming thirty-something character from *up North*. But in reality Crazy Horse, as he is better known, is part of the underbelly of the hard-man scene, hailing from an industrial area where the populous were rather bizarrely labelled 'Monkey Hangers' ... Hartlepool.

This curious title was supposedly bestowed upon the close-knit community after a monkey was mistakenly identified as a spy and promptly hanged. The monkey-hanging incident is said to have happened during the Napoleonic Wars, and could be put down to the fishing community never having seen a monkey before. The fishermen of Hartlepool watched as a French vessel sank off the Hartlepool coast during a storm. The only survivor of the wreck was the ship's pet monkey, apparently dressed to amuse the forlorn crew in a military style uniform. Fearing that this monkey was either a French infiltrator or spy, the fishermen, so the story goes, questioned the monkey and held a makeshift trial on the beach. After a fruitless interrogation of the so-called Frenchman, the conclusion was that this monkey was, indeed, a French spy and was summarily sentenced to death by hanging. Quite appropriately, the monkey was despatched to its death at the end of a rope from the mast of a fishing boat.

As much as the story about the monkey is legendary, so is the story about Hartlepool's living legend, Richy Horsley, Crazy Horse, but even more so.

With such a character as 'Dodgy' Dave Courtney, the Monarch of the Underworld, contributing the foreword to Crazy Horse's book and tributes from the likes of Roy Shaw and Charles Bronson (UK prisoner), this shows how well known Crazy Horse has become. This popularity that Crazy Horse has within both the hard-man fraternity and their followers, north and south, reveals a true warrior.

Selected to play the film role of an American boxer who fights the former unlicensed heavyweight boxing champ of Great Britain, Roy Shaw, in the proposed biographical film about the late real-life hard man Lenny McLean – *The Guv'nor* – is a further indication of Richy's popularity.

This is testimony to Crazy Horse's current status, and lends itself to the thought that he should have his own story told in full ... and here, in his own words, Richy tells it as it is.

CHAPTER 1

CIRCLE OF LIFE

Never judge a book by its cover. Take my childhood: judging by my present record of violence, you would think that I was brought up in an abattoir, but you would be wrong. I came from a happy home, where my parents lavished me with love. There was no family brutality of any sort. I recall being told from an early age that I was miraculously found under a gooseberry bush, which to some extent wasn't as far removed from the truth as it may sound.

When I reached the age of five, I was told I had been adopted as a baby. At that time I was gun and holster mad, a bit of a lone ranger, as was the rage in those days. My parents, Tom and Brenda, told me that when they saw a number of kids for adoption, they picked me out as being special. They waited apprehensively for my reaction, but

I just looked up and chimed, 'Did I have my guns on?' That's how life was back then ... not so long ago!

My childhood memories are fond ones, which every kid should be able to experience. My mother always instilled a sense of self-worth and paved the way ahead by showing me what respect for my elders was all about. I remember, for instance, jumping up and down in a muddy puddle at the age of five, absolutely covered in clarts of mud from head to toe. An old lady from down the road walked past and saw the state of disorder I was in. She gasped, 'Richard, look at the state of you, your mam will go mad!' Now don't ask me where my reply came from, but I looked at her and fumed, 'Fuck off!' Of course, Mam found out and took me to the old dear's house and forced me to apologise. Mam always presented me to the world in a clean and tidy fashion ... oh, and I always wore shorts! Not many hard bastards can say that about their childhoods.

Yet even though my parents treated me with the best care, it didn't take long for me to discover the world of pain for myself. I recall an incident in the summer of that year when Bobbin, a good friend of my mam's, took me to Crimdon Dene, a nearby holiday town, for the day. Bobbin's real name was Anne, but I renamed her because she used to play a game with me called 'Roll-a-Bobbin'. That name, Bobbin, has stuck – even after hitting sixty! It had been an exciting and tiring day, but when we arrived back home at teatime I still wanted to be out with my friends. After thanking Bobbin and saying my goodbyes, I paused outside the door, stupidly resting my fingers on the door frame. But Mam thought I'd gone out and closed the door. My dear late mam, to her shock, heard the CRUNCH, followed by my screaming. When she prised open the door, she saw me stood there with my finger end hanging off, blood and gore everywhere!

This was my first introduction to real pain and it showed me that I could be hurt ... a valuable lesson at an early age, but not one that I would recommend! I was rushed to the hospital and had the end of my finger stitched back on. This of course was in the days before microsurgery. The doctors did the best they could, a good job given the circumstances, but I was left with a disfigured finger end, a stark reminder as to how vulnerable we all are.

I was lucky, as my parents never overreacted when I got into scrapes. Take, for instance, my first drinking experience non New Year's Day, 1970. There was a drinks table in the corner of the living room, full of bottles of sherry. Mam asked Bobbin to watch over me and to see to it that I didn't touch any of the drinks when her and Dad went into the kitchen to cook. Of course, with the seasonal festivities, Bobbin was a bit tired and had a stonker of a hangover from the night before, and soon fell fast asleep on the couch. On seeing this, I edged closer and closer towards the table. Like the

3

male dancer in the Guinness advert, I contorted and twisted myself in order to avoid making any unnecessary noise as I slithered towards my prize. Eventually, after a few nimble moves, I reached my destination, and sat down contently at the table. I swiftly helped myself to a bottle of QC sherry. After guzzling most of it down, I was rewarded by becoming utterly and completely pissed out of my mind.

I started stumbling all over the place whilst laughing my intoxicated head off. On hearing this commotion, Mam came into the room, pointed at me and said, 'What's the matter with him?' She spotted the half empty bottle of QC sherry on the floor at the exact same time as Bobbin was awakened by my shenanigans and realised what was happening. She pleaded, 'I'm sorry, I'm sorry!'

Mam cried out, 'He'll have to go to the hospital now!'

But Dad calmly said, 'Put him to bed and let him sleep it off.'

And that's what they did. My mother was beside herself with worry in case I choked on vomit, and was constantly doing bed watch on me every ten minutes, but they never overreacted. When I came back down later on, I was rough and hung over for the rest of the day, but at least it gave me an appetite, as I ate all my cooked dinner, a miracle for me as I was a very bad eater. I was practically brought up on Ready Brek and Minodex multi-vitamins.

At that time, the Weegram family lived next door to us. They had a son called Donald who was also my age and a firm friend. He was a fellow explorer of the world of pain. One day in 1969 we were playing a game to see how high we could throw darts into the air. Well, Donald propelled one up high, forgetting Isaac Newton's Law of Gravity. It shot back down, heading straight for me. The dart hit me like a bullet from a gun – not that I knew the feeling, at least not at that age! I ran into the house, a screaming human dartboard. I was in shock, painful shock, with a dart sticking out of my neck. I must have looked like the son of William Tell. I remember thinking to myself, was this it, was this how death was?

Another time, Donald and me were in my bedroom while his mam, Hilary, was having a cuppa downstairs. Normally we were very noisy, but on this particular day we were unusually quiet. When Hilary was ready to leave, she and my parents decided to come upstairs to see why we were being so quiet. They opened the door and were met by quite a sight: me and Donald standing with knitting needles in our hands, surrounded by the shreds of wallpaper which we had innocently stripped from half the bedroom walls! Oh heck! I thought I was in for it, but instead of going mad they just laughed their heads off … great memories. Not long after this little incident, the Weegram family moved to the other side of town and I was gutted to have to say goodbye to my pal Donald.

I suppose you could say I had been acquainted with pain from the beginning. I'd been suffering on and off with an earache and blocked-nose problem since I was a baby, but the hospital wouldn't take me in for the operation until I was at least five years old. The problem went away for a while, but returned when I was six, so they thought it time to give me the op. By this age I'd been at war with a door and acted as a pincushion for a dart, nah ... this wouldn't hurt me one bit!

The first thing I was given to eat after I had the dreaded tonsils and adenoids out was a welcoming bowl of custard. An easy experience, I was beginning to think. But when I took my first gulp of custard, I immediately recoiled away from the spoon, feeling that someone had let loose a million wasps in my throat, with their stings coated with lemon juice for good measure! I was mollycoddled in hospital for four days. Nowadays they try to get you in and out within a day because they need the bed space.

Even though I was out discovering things for myself, I still learned a lot from my dad's experiences, which he often told me about. When my dad was growing up there was a bully who thought he could take on the world. He used to pick fights and loved people cowering in his presence, getting satisfaction from intimidating people. There was one man he harassed in particular, who was always out exercising, jogging and skipping. Every time the bully saw him out jogging he would call him a 'Big

Nancy' and a 'Fairy' and tell him what he could do to him, but the guy just used to laugh and take no notice. So one day, on spotting the guy skipping outside, the bully decided it was about time he gave him a good hiding. Now those were the days when they used to fight inside a drawn circle, just using their fists like real men should. The rules were simple: you couldn't step outside the circle unless you'd had enough or were carried out. The bully and the guy he had been abusing quickly drew a crowd around their circle as they started battling it out. The bully's inflated ego dramatically burst as he received the whipping of his life. He was humiliated in front of everyone. He had been taught a double lesson: to stop bullying and never to judge a book by its cover.

Some people have never experienced violence, never had a fight in their lives, and couldn't knock the crust off a rice pudding. I, too, was a fight virgin, but the time for me to lose my virginity was looming.

An older and bigger kid who lived around the corner was always intimidating me, my first real experience of being bullied. Don't these bullies always live around the corner from you? I would often find myself running for home, crying my eyes out after being attacked by him. One day my parents gave me an easy solution to this dilemma when they said to me, 'Stop running in crying all the time and learn to stick up for yourself.' That was all very well for an adult but, to a child's mind, this lad was the equivalent of a two-ton rhinoceros.

7

It was a lovely day outside, and I remember that Mam and Dad were sat on the doorstep enjoying the sunshine. I went back outside and walked up to the street corner where the bully was. From a safe distance and within the protective earshot and sight of my parents, I did what most bullied kids would do: I shouted and goaded him with a few choice names, which was like a red rag to a bull. As the bullying rhino charged towards me, I ran to the safety of my parents. When he saw my mam and dad sat on the step he stopped running and slowed to a walk. But as he loomed towards me something came over me, and for a change I was the one who saw red.

I don't know if it was because I knew I had the Seventh Cavalry behind me in the form of my parents, but all fear left me. The tables had turned. The hunter became the hunted. I started walking towards him with an air of confidence in my step. As soon as he was in striking distance, I hit him with a haymaker of a punch, catching him right on the ear! I stood there with my fists clenched, ready for more, just staring at him with anger emanating from my eyes. I can remember the pain etched on his face and the tears of fear in his eyes as he turned away from me and traipsed off into the distance, holding his head to one side, a memory that still gives me satisfaction.

I was amazed at what I'd just done! I had slain my dragon and overcome my fear. Needless to say, he never bullied me again. I could have very well said that my parents threatened me with a beating if I didn't face up to my fear, but that wasn't the case. I faced the bully myself ... admittedly with a little help from Mam and Dad sat on the step. That was the first time I performed in front of a crowd, albeit a non-paying one. As I grew older and fought more fights, I became increasingly used to the watchful crowd.

CHAPTER 2

TANK THE BLEEDER

The first day I met Tommy, he said to me in half English, half German that he was going to stab me. This, I thought, was strange behaviour for a five-year-old. Tommy's family had just moved into one of the council houses opposite us.

Friendships can spring from the most surprising of places and situations and, as I said, never judge a book by its cover. We became best of friends and even started our first day at school together at Grange Primary. Our mothers also became best friends. One day they dropped us both off at school before going off to the local shops. Assured in the knowledge that we were safely in school, they shopped to their hearts' content, until they got home and spotted Tommy and me sitting on the front doorstep. We had done a runner from school, but hadn't been too bright by running straight home instead of off to the local park. To this day, I still see Tommy and we remain friends. And he hasn't stabbed me yet! When I think about it, I feel old because we have been friends since the 1960s. What started out as confrontation ended up as a lasting friendship.

Tommy's sister Donna came into the world in 1969. Her mam told me that, one day, when Donna was about four months old, she was in her pram and I put my finger in her hand. She squeezed it so tight, I couldn't get it free. She wouldn't let me go and I had to call for her mam, who prized my finger out from her clenched fist. I think she was trying to tell me something. We've always been very close – you could say we were soulmates. I was at her Christening and she was a bridesmaid at Mam's wedding. She is an absolute diamond.

My inspiration for boxing must stem from my Granda Morris, my mam's father. Granda was an ex-boxer, known in his time as Sonny 'Kid' Morris. I remember one occasion when I visited his house and started fun fighting in the garden with my cousin Michael, whose nickname, as it happened, was Tank. Well, Tank was older than me, and I guess he wanted to play rough. I got on top of him and he said, 'Do you want a real fight or a fun fight, it doesn't bother me.' Whether he said it to make me think, No way, I don't want a real fight with you, you're the Guv'nor, or whether he just had a rush of testosterone, I don't know. I started hesitating, saying, 'Er ... em,' and looked at my dad, who was also in the garden, laughing.

Tank started repeating, 'I'm not bothered, I will, it doesn't make any difference to me.' Then, in a split second, my mind changed. I focused in on the target – his head – and shouted, 'REAL FIGHT!' I released a burst of about ten punches, all of them slamming home into Tank's face with the precision of an Exocet missile: left, right, left, right. Now Tank was a bleeder – he could bleed for England. He was always having nosebleeds and today was to be no exception: there was claret everywhere! We both got a telling-off and were told make up. But when I looked at my dad, he was grinning from ear to ear.

A couple of years later, Tank got into trouble with a friend of mine called Anth. Now Anth was a boxer and a tough kid: he could take care of himself. When Tank told me he was going to fight him, I thought to myself, He is underestimating Anth and is in for a shock. I watched the fight and within seconds Tank's nose was bust! Anth was getting the better of it. Tank changed tactics and took him to the floor. As they were grappling on the deck, Tank started scooping up the blood from his nose and rubbed it into Anth's eyes so he couldn't see; that's when they got split up. Both claimed outright victory but nobody actually won. Anth was in five national boxing finals as a junior, only one of which he won, but he had some bad decisions given against him.

Years later he was my corner man at some of my fights, but I never bled on him like Tank did!

There's something quite different about fighting at school that can bring the worst out of kids. Whether it's showing off to your peers or just bravado, it sure is different compared to any other type of fighting. My first fight at school was with a lad known as Smiler. He was a big lump of a lad with short hair, who was much stronger than me and had the look of a Rottweiler in his eye. The fight resulted from a fun fight turned serious – as usual, it started when none of us would back out. I remember the lad rushing me like a raging bull. Each time he got close, I would unleash a barrage of punches at him to keep him at a distance. He was stronger than me and if he got me down to the ground I probably wouldn't have been able to get him off. My heart was pounding as hard as a bongo drum trying to break out of my chest. This was for real, with the result that fear had turned my legs to jelly with the adrenalin rush. He kept charging, I kept throwing punches back. Eventually a vigilant teacher in the playground broke it up. There was blood all over my hands and legs, all of it from the raging bull's nose. Not that I had it all my own way: I sported a black eye for the next week, and received a severe ticking-off from the Head. But at least I didn't spill any of my own blood!

Not long after that, a relation of mine called Tina, who was also a Horsley, started getting picked on by a lad at school. Why lads want to pick on girls, I'll never know. I mean, it's not a macho thing to do. In fact if there's one thing I hate more than bullies, it is men who abuse women. One playtime Tina asked me if I would tell this lad to leave her alone, and pointed out the coward to me. In a flash, I grabbed hold of him, pointed towards Tina, and spat out at him through gritted teeth, 'She's my cousin, so leave her alone.' To finish the matter I then gave him a taste of his own medicine: a few well-aimed punches and kicks, something for him to remember. He certainly never touched Tina again, but then again, he's probably ended up married to some punch bag of woman with no-one to stick up for her.

Dad was also a good fighter in his younger days. He had his own tag, 'Blood Horsley'. He kept many of his friendships from his fighting days throughout his life, such as 'The Battler', a street fighter of yesteryear who was Hartlepool's first bouncer. He had 19 pro fights as a heavyweight boxer back in the early 1930s and was said to be some character. Back in the thirties, times were really hard for the working classes and many people had to fight just to put food on the table. Pubs were full of people who were down on their luck and drowning their sorrows so it was no wonder they had people like The Battler minding the door – trouble was often only a whisper away. Bear in mind that Hartlepool was also a dock, so we had people from all over the world docking here and drinking in the pubs. You had to be tough to survive.

Fighting, though, wasn't my only preoccupation in those days. I was also embedded in family life. I had a step-brother and two step-sisters for a start. Dad had originally married a girl called Lil from West Auckland, with whom he had three children: Helen, John and Ruth. She had also been pregnant with twins, but had miscarried when she fell down the stairs. She later died tragically of TB. As a result, my dad's mam, Granny Horsley, brought up Helen, John and Ruth as Dad was away working. He grafted all over the country. That was back in the days when you could start a job in the morning and piss off at dinnertime if you didn't like it – you could go and find another one the next day. After a while, though, he took a permanent job at the local paper mill so he could be with the kids more.

In late 1970, Mam found out that she had cervical cancer. She went into hospital for a biopsy and didn't get out until Christmas Eve. They had wanted her to stay, but she wanted to be home for Christmas so things could be as normal as possible. Three weeks later, Mam went into Newcastle General Hospital to have intense radiotherapy treatment. She was in there for a full month. I can remember going up there on the train with my dad and my mam's sister, Auntie Ellen, to visit her. One time after seeing her, Dad was sick in the street. Mam then got transferred to Hartlepool where she stayed for two more weeks and had a full hysterectomy operation. After that, she had to go for regular screening every six weeks for a year, until it lessened to a screening every six months for two years. Eventually she got the all-clear. And I thought tonsillitis was bad! Pretty hard times, but it goes to show that there can be a pot of gold at the end of the rainbow of despair ... my mam proved it, a tough lady to the end.

As bad as this episode was, it did get me closer to Dad's other kids, as I used to stay at Granny Horsley's house when Dad went to Newcastle to visit Mam. My older step-brother John lived at Gran's, and he used to take me to the park a lot to feed the ducks and the geese. We also used to take out Gran's mongrel dog, Kim, for long walks. She lived to the good old age of 16. I used to tell Kim to 'STAY' while I walked halfway round the block before shouting at the top of my voice, 'HOWAY, KIM, HOWAY!' I would then run as fast as I could to see if I could get back to Gran's first, but Kim always caught me. That was also a period in which I became obsessed with Donald Duck. Out of all the Disney characters, he was my favourite and I had a big sticker of him on my headboard, and Dad had bought me a cap gun and a football imprinted with his picture. You might say I was a bit quackers! I still watch the odd cartoon, but what really takes me back to those days is music. Gran used to have the wireless on, and there are some records that always take me back to those days when I hear them. Records like Marc Bolan's 'Ride A White Swan' – who can forget that classic? And George Harrison's 'My

Sweet Lord', which was Number One at the time and was forever being played on the radio.

CHAPTER 3

FISTS OF FURY

They say revenge is a dish best served cold. Unfortunately for me, this was literally the case when I encountered my first junior school bully. I had just entered the first year, and was one day sitting down to eat my dinner, when the resident bully homed in on some new prey, and fired a mouthful of spit on my plate. There was no segregation or special privileges for first-year kids in those days – we had to eat our dinner with the rest of the school, meaning that this little incident was likely to repeat itself again and again. I'm not ashamed to say that at that age I was scared shitless and didn't dare say boo to a goose, at least not to this bully, who was three years above me. I kept quiet about it and didn't even tell my parents, but such silence inevitably starts the ball rolling, and soon enough your pretending to have a stomach ache

19

or various other medical problems in order to get out of going to school.

It kept on happening. It must have made the fucking pig feel tough, even though he was picking on someone much younger than himself. Eventually I told my parents. Like my initial scrap with the bully on the street corner, I enlisted their help to take yet another bully's scalp. My parents were good friends with the family of an older lad at the school called 'Collo'. His real name was Michael Collins and, like his famous Irish namesake, he knew how to have a scrap. Dad must have said something as he came back the same night and instructed me to go over to Collo tomorrow at playtime, tell him who I was, and point out the lad picking on me. He went on to say that Collo's father would be putting Collo wise as to the situation. The next day, at morning break, I looked for Collo because I couldn't bear the thought of another dinner with spit in it. I certainly needed to beef myself up, but at this rate I was slimming down like a national WeightWatchers champion! I spotted Collo in the schoolyard and went over to see him.

'Hi,' I blurted out, 'I'm Richard and my dad was at your house about someone spitting in my dinner.'

He replied, 'I know, show me who he is.' We looked around the yard. I spotted him instantly and yelled out to Collo, 'THERE HE IS!'

The tables had been turned against my predator.

Collo ran over and grabbed him. He pointed at me and then growled in his face, 'If I were you, I would stop picking on him. And don't ever spit in his dinner again.' Then followed an unmerciful beating. And I mean unmerciful. Collo gave the bully one hell of a savage walloping, and practically kicked him from one end of the yard to the other. You should have heard the pig scream! Excuse the pun, but I can only admit that the bully got his just desserts. Nevertheless, while this should have filled me with happiness, I could only feel like shit, as I felt like I had been the cause of it all. Then again, Mam and Dad were glad when I told them what had happened. If Collo ever reads this, I'd just like to say 'thank you', you did me a big favour. By taking out this bully, you allowed me to eat all my dinners undisturbed!

As a general rule I can't tolerate bullies, but I guess you could say that even fairly solid people have a tendency to do the odd bit of bullying. There was a lad called David who lived at the end of our block, who used to bully a kid called Tommy from over the road. David kept on calling him names, nothing physical mind, but then again, these were some nasty names! David didn't realise, however, that Tommy had a boiling point, which he hit one day after a flurry of insults. Tommy had had enough. The lid on the pressure cooker blew right off. He ran over the road like a madman and started laying into David, ramming home a flurry of fists in his face. David ended up in tears, but he did learn a valuable lesson that day. To my knowledge he never picked on or underestimated anyone ever again.

After that little lesson, David and I got to be good friends. We used to ride our bikes together around the neighbourhood. This wasn't long after the film *Easy Rider*, which exerted quite a bit of influence on me, and instilled a longing for a Harley Davidson chopper motorcycle. I wanted to imagine myself as one of the film's lead characters, either Wyatt or Billy, played respectively by the excellent Peter Fonda and Dennis Hopper. The closest I got to realise this dream was back in 1971 when the Chopper bicycle was the craze throughout the nation. The big padded seat was comfortable for your backside, and even had gears! It really didn't take a big stretch of the imagination to think of yourself as one of the gang from *Easy Rider* on a Harley. Every time that I saw someone riding a Chopper, I just used to stare at the bike and wish that it were mine. Luckily for me, I didn't have to wait too long.

Christmas mornings followed a familiar pattern in our house. Just as the sun was rising, my mam and dad would shout up to me from downstairs to look out of the window. They'd shout, 'There's Santa.' Dad would ring a bell and pretend that it was the sound from Santa's sleigh.

I would excitedly jump out of bed, and look out of the

bedroom window into the dark morning, fully expecting to see Santa and his reindeers magically flying through the air. Maybe he would even spot me and give a wave. 'I can't see him,' I'd proclaim in sadness. Then the bells would stop. He must have gone to someone else's house, I would think, but I also knew that he hadn't forgotten me. I'd run downstairs and into the room whilst still in my pyjamas, and start opening the prezzies. The excitement was unbelievable and my parents used to buzz as they watched my face beaming up at them in joy.

This Christmas, however, was slightly different. I was playing with my presents when my parents told me to go into the kitchen to see what I wanted for breakfast. 'You just pick me something,' I snapped, but they insisted I had a look. I rushed to the kitchen just to get this chore out of the way so that I could get back to my prezzies. 'I'll have Ready Bre ...' I was then frozen in my tracks by the sight of something that I shall never forget! There it stood in its entire glory, gleaming, brand spanking new and blue. This was the present I had been dreaming of, the one I had asked Santa for in my letter to him, but never thought I'd actually get. A Chopper bike! There was a card attached to it that read: 'From Mam, Dad and Santa'. I wanted to jump straight on it and go out for a ride but Mam and Dad said, 'Have some breakfast first, and then get ready.'

Were they kidding or what, have some breakfast first?

I couldn't wait to get out on it and show it off to the other kids. I gulped down my brekkie, and rushed out the door on my Chopper. I went straight over to David's, eager for him to see my new Chopper, so that he'd wish that he could have one just like it too. David's door opened and I waited in anticipation for him to come out. He came out first and then his dad followed with ... David's new bike! When I saw it, I nearly fell off mine. I couldn't believe it. It was a brand spanking new gleaming blue replica of my Chopper! What? He had one too! They were so similar that you couldn't tell them apart. In the end, David's dad got him some stickers with his name on in order to tell the two bikes apart so that we would stop fighting over whose bike was whose.

This, however, did not put an end to our fighting. One day we each had a rope with a knot in the end, which we started swinging at each other with complete abandonment. The idea was to try and land first blood. We were aiming full-blooded swings at each other, gradually getting closer to the target. Then BANG! I caught him square in the face with my knot. The screaming soon followed, and his dad came out and took him inside for much-needed medical attention. We didn't fight much after that. As I went home victorious, I knew I wouldn't be having any trouble with him again.

CHAPTER 4

HONOUR AND PRIDE

Some things never change. Sport will always exert a big influence on boys, and I was no different. My love affair with football began when I was six. My dad would take shots at me with a football on the grass outside our house. I loved being a goalkeeper, owing in the main to my idolisation of the current England goalie, Gordon Banks. I had a big scrapbook dedicated to him. Dad got in on the act too, as every time he took a shot he would shout, 'Save this one, Banksie.' I was shattered when Banksie lost an eye in a car accident in 1972, at the height of his abilities, when he was undoubtedly the world's number one. He did try to make a comeback in America for a time, but later said that he felt like a bit of a circus act: 'Roll up, roll up! The world's only one-eyed goalkeeper.' And so he retired from football for good. If he wanted another eye, all he had to do was ask and he could have had one of mine. That's how much I idolised him.

All that practice with my dad eventually paid off, as by the time I was eight I had become an established goalkeeper, and was probably the best in the town for my age. Halfway through my first year at junior school, my parents sent me to another school, as they thought it offered a better education. My new school had a great football culture, where everyone would turn up to watch the 'A' team play – always a real occasion. The strip was light blue with a white hoop around the neck and wrist, light-blue shorts and socks – a Manchester City lookalike strip. The goalkeeper's jersey, which I longed to wear, was solid black. My good performances in sports lessons quickly got noticed, and I didn't have to wait long to break into the side.

By the time I entered the third year, I was getting games for both the 'A' and 'B' teams. And luck had it that my first game for the 'A' team was against my former school. This turned out to be a good baptism for me, and we came away with a 2-2 draw. Strangely enough, we played each other again a few days later when our 'B' teams met. The opposition started moaning as soon as they realised that I had played in the earlier game for the 'A' team. We argued back that the only reason I had played then was because the normal goalie was sick, which they accepted. Maybe they should have been more resistant, as we stuffed them 3-0!

Our school was Protestant, but right next to us there was a Catholic school, Saint Teresa's. They, too, had an excellent football team, and were our bitter rivals. Needless to say, it was always a big game when we met them. Both teams wanted to win so badly – this wasn't just a football match, it was a case of upholding honour and pride. I only ever played in one derby game. On that occasion we didn't have a full team because some of our players were out with the flu. The St Teresa's coach came over and mocked us, bleating, 'I thought you were supposed to have a good team, your school?' This was quite a provocation, so we rushed to the homes of our absent team members and begged them to play. We just managed to get a squad together. We returned to the pitch, where a good crowd had built up. As it was at their place, everyone was anticipating a Teresa's win against an under-strength Rossmere.

The first half was very even, with both sides creating scoring chances. The difference was they couldn't get anything past me. We were more clinical, and went into the half-time break 1-0 up. There was only one team in it in the second half, as they played us off the field. The pressure on us was relentless. Adding to this was the fact that the ref was also their coach; he slipped on an extra ten minutes. This paid off, as they equalised with the last kick of the game. They had got out of jail by the skin of their teeth. Our coach ran over screaming at theirs and called him a cheat for finding an extra ten minutes from nowhere.

My love of football continued to keep me busy when I became a fan of our local team, Hartlepool United. Our Ruth's husband, Dave, took me to some of their home games. Dave and his mates used to go every week and stand in the same place. They used to get right into it and gave the opposition players lots of verbal abuse. Although I followed Hartlepool United, Leeds United was my main time at that time. Mam and Dad were friends with a couple called Harry and Jean, who lived down the bottom of our street. Harry was a rough old sod, and used to grab me whenever we went to see them and give me a good tussle. To make things worse, he was a big Sunderland fan, a team Leeds played in the 1973 FA Cup final. Harry would scowl and blast torments at me, calling Leeds crap, bigging-up Sunderland, that kind of banter. Well, my nightmare was complete when Sunderland won the final 1-0. Five minutes later, there was a letter delivered to our house addressed to me. When I opened it, it read: 'SUNDERLAND 1'. Underneath that in very small letters: 'Leeds 0'. No prizes for guessing who had sent it.

What else influenced me as I was growing up? Well, certainly the community spirit of the 1970s. It might sound clichéd, but people did use to leave their doors unlocked. Then again, that could have been down to the fact that there wasn't much worth nicking! That community spirit still exists in Hartlepool, and above all in me, since its values have stayed with me. People cared for each other, and the family was the centre of your life. Like my mam and dad, my mother's friend Annie Bobbin and her husband couldn't have kids. In 1976 she finally became a mother when her and Jimmy adopted a beautiful baby girl, whom they called Joanne. When Annie went to pick her up and bring her home, my mam and Ken went along with her. She was a lovely child and never wanted for anything – in fact, she was spoilt rotten. When she was in her teens, she was diagnosed with kidney trouble and had to go on dialysis. We were all devastated. Eventually, she stopped the treatment and failed to turn up for her appointments. Obviously, this took its toll and, tragically, she died the week before Christmas in 2001.

Meanwhile, I had more family through my Aunt Lois, who was married to a Polish man called Bob Gers. They had four children, the oldest of whom, Janick – pronounced Yanick – was constantly playing his guitar. All he did was practise, practise, practise. I remember one day hearing him playing Rod Stewart's 'Maggie May' in the front room, and realising just how good he was becoming. Janick was only young then himself. He played in a few bands, with Fish from Marillion and Ian Gillan from Deep Purple. He was such a brilliant player that it didn't take long for him to get his first big break, when he got an audition for Iron Maiden. As soon as they heard our Jan play, they knew he was the man they wanted. He's now world famous himself and has been on numerous world tours. He played on the Number One hit single 'Bring Your Daughter To The Slaughter'. His hard work paid off. No one deserved it more: a real down-to-earth family man.

Janick especially respected my dad – he once told me that he thought the world of him. Not long after the Leeds defeat, Dad was taken ill, which certainly put things in perspective for me. The hospital tests diagnosed him as suffering from kidney failure. He had to go in for dialysis three times a week. Mam went to the hospital with him and stayed for the full ten hours, so she could get trained on using the dialysis machine. At that time, we were still living in a two-bedroom house, and had to apply for a three-bedroom house so that one of the rooms could be made into a dialysis room. We eventually moved into a three-bedroom house, which made life a lot easier for Mam and Dad as they didn't have to do all the travelling to the hospital. Then again, one good thing did come of it all: a sister on the ward had a brother who was in the Leeds United Supporters Club, who got me some memorabilia signed by the Leeds striker Allan Clarke.

It wasn't much longer before I attended my first big game at St James's Park, the home of Newcastle United. Jim McKie, a great bloke from Scotland who was Tina's father, the girl I stopped from getting bullied, took me and Tank to see a game against Leeds on Boxing Day 1973. I couldn't wait. The crowds were unreal; I'd never seen this many people in my life. We queued for what seemed like an eternity – I'd seen a dole queue move faster than this. For some reason, Jim had asked his mate to look after us, and said he'd see us after the match. Just before we got to the entrance, the bloke at the turnstile shouted, 'No More! The ground's full.' I was devastated! What could we do now? Suddenly we spotted another way in. I slipped my way through and all of a sudden, there they were! My heroes in the flesh, who I'd only seen on telly and in the papers before now. I was in awe, dumbstruck at seeing them in the flesh!

I took a moment to behold the sight I was seeing amid the pushing and shoving legions of football fanatics. The threat that violence could erupt at any moment was prevailing – you could smell it in the air. I watched Ian McFaul, the Magpies' goalkeeper, who was featured on the opening credits of TV's premier football programme *Match of the Day* for a while. Then I kept an eye on the Leeds goalkeeper, David Harvey, analysing how he masterfully controlled his back four. After a while though, the section we were in got too crowded, so Tank and I prised ourselves out and headed into the streets of Newcastle. We just walked and talked, always checking that we didn't stray too far from the ground. Darkness descended early and, as full-time approached, we made our way back towards the ground. Leeds had won 1-0 from a goal by Paul Madeley. The pubs were quickly filling up, with heaps of empty Newcastle Brown Ale bottles strewn across the pavements. After about 15 minutes, we spotted Jim, who looked harassed and very glad to see us.

Football wasn't the only sport I was interested in. I used to love the school sports days. I remember one in particular when I competed in the 200-metre sprint. It was a lovely day. As soon as the starting pistol went, I shot off like a rocket. My heart, legs and lungs were on fire! Coming into the home strait my lead was drastically reduced. As a few started to pass me on the run-in, I collapsed in a heap exhausted, eventually finishing last. Yeah, I sure showed them what a fool I was.

So I didn't win the race, but at least I was good with a baseball bat. Those were the when days I used a baseball for just playing rounders, not as a weapon of defence. We all loved playing rounders. I think I might have made a baseball player if I was a young lad living in the USA. I was also pretty handy at cricket, but sometimes my fielding left a bit to be desired. One game, my friend Tony I'anson whacked a ball my way – either I would catch it or it would go for six. In a split second, I decided to go for a spectacular catch and dived as if I was in goal. Then there was a mighty thud as the cork ball hit me smack in the eye. Instant pain isn't the word! I might as well have been hit with a jackhammer. I had an absolute peach of a shiner that lasted for a while.

Despite all this fun, the future for some of us wasn't to be too rosy. Years later, Tony got in with a wild crowd, and ended up going on an armed robbery. The police were there waiting, since one of their so-called pals had grassed on them. Tony got a nice twelve-and-a-half year stretch for his troubles. He kept his head down and served his jail sentence like a man, but it should never have happened. But I guess we never know what the future holds.

CHAPTER 5

FIGHTING LIKE A LION

I bet you're wondering what the hell is going on. You've bought this book expecting tales of family beatings, awful poverty, and whatever else goes into the making of a true fighter. Well, don't worry, the fighting will come along soon enough. But like I say, I had a loving upbringing, so that when I ask myself why I become a warrior, I can only answer: I was born one.

I had always been an active kid. From 1971–74, I was best of pals with four mates that I had met whilst kicking my Donald Duck ball against a wall outside Gran's house. Me, Trev, Rob, Kev and Mick were all football mad – Rob was so talented a player that we all expected him to turn pro, but sadly he never did. We used to go to parks to see who was playing football. We challenged various groups 'us against yous' stuff, the first team to ten wins. We never lost a single game. We also went all over on our bikes, and played games like 'Kick The Tin' and 'British Bulldogs', which are absolute classics. I hear the government are on about introducing these games back into schools to try and instil some old values and to get the kids fit. Personally, I think it would be like asking them to wear shoulder pads in their wide-lapelled jackets and to put on platform boots – it just can't work! Not only that, but there is too much promiscuity and lawlessness about today for kids to be interested in those games. To change people's values would mean changing the whole scene around us. Nah, forget it! Overall though, it's a shame that era has gone, as those were some of the happiest times of my life.

That, however, is not to say that I stopped fighting, far from it. Once there was a bit of trouble when Rob booted me in the face and broke my nose. It was a bit of a scuffle, nothing more, and we soon sorted it out. In fact I can't even recall what it was over! I could take a good shot even when I was eight – something, of course, that has never left me, as there's a video of one of my later fights where I take 94 clean punches to the head and am still standing at the final bell. By the time I was ten, I'd had about fifteen fights, and almost all of them were over after a few punches, which is common to most street fights. I started to develop my own style, which was based on one vital lesson: always expect the unexpected. Complacency is another Achilles heel. I remember once fighting the son of a karate specialist, who thought he was the bee's knees. I totally wiped the floor with him, messed him up something proper. His old man was supposed to be making an appearance at my uncle's house, but never turned up – he must have decided to stay at home with a pork chop!

I was always a quiet lad, so people used to think I wasn't up to much, but when they saw me go to work with my fists they quickly changed their minds. I was getting involved in arranged fights as early as the age of eight, when I was involved in a scrap outside the local baths. I can remember it exactly: I turn around to walk a few metres to get some distance from my opponent before we begin. I can hear whispering. The next thing I know, some lad jumps me from behind, and starts to choke me. Luckily, I manage to get him off, and hurl him to the floor. Next thing I know I'm on top of him, smashing punches into his face like a steam hammer. It was all over. Less than 15 seconds from start to finish! Why hang about in long, drawn-out fights? You want them to be over as quick as possible. Fortunately, I was blessed with a pitiless punch that sorted the men out from the boys. The only drawback to having such a vicious punch is that I have often broken my hands over the years.

Sometimes it's hard to keep out of trouble. There was a family in the early 1970s who lived opposite my

Granda Morris, who were always having scraps with my cousin Kevin, Tank's brother. Well, one day I was watching one of these fights through the window when I saw Kevin get jumped by the older brother, just as Kevin was finishing off one of the younger ones. He started knocking the hell out of Kevin. My sense of fair play kicked in, and I charged out, tore into the oldest brother and gave him a bloody good hiding. I destroyed him! That beating, however, didn't settle things, and I ended up having about four fights with this prat over time. I chinned him every time! Eventually he learned his lesson.

Just as I was coming of age as a fighter, my Granda, Sonny 'Kid' Morris, passed away. He had been a damn good amateur back in his day. He had beaten one lad three times who went on to become the British, Empire and European Champion as a professional. Granda's professional career, however, wasn't as impressive as his amateur one; he had 16 pro fights – 5 wins, 9 losses and 2 draws. Still, his pro record is opposite for anyone interested. Thanks to Miles Templeton, who provided me with it.

Granda died of a heart attack. I can still remember when I heard my mam crying just after she had heard.

My Uncle Keith, who was our Kev's dad, had come around to give the bad news. He was a coalman who had his own business. He had lads out delivering coal for him. I'd go out collecting coal money with them. We'd

PRO RECORD OF KID MORRIS

1932
Dec. 23	Boy Adams	L R3

1933
Jan.	Young Adams	Drew 4
Jun. 16	Boy Thomas	W pts 6
Sep. 15	Kid Adams	W pts 6

1934
Jul. 20	Teddy Baker	Drew 4
Sep. 16	Kid Adams	L KO 3
Nov. 23	Dick Measor	W pts 4

1935
May 3	Kid Measor	pts 4

1936
Aug. 14	Young Catcher	W KO 3

1937
Aug. 5	Kid Henderson	L pts 6
Aug. 30	Billy Coburn	L KO 1

1938
Jun. 13	Tom Rush	W KO 3
Jun. 20	Jack Dennis	L pts 6
Jul. 11	Boy O'Shea	L pts 6
Jul. 28	Billy Coburn	L KO 1
Sep. 15	Jacky Rogers	L KO 2

be out a couple of hours at night and would get 50p each – cushty in those days! Other times, Keith would come home drunk as a skunk and would give all of us kids handfuls of money – and we would think we were rich.

As you can see, I had a big family, and can remember quite a bit about them. However, when it comes to saying why us Horsleys settled in Hartlepool, I'm afraid I can't give you a definite answer. I do know that the first Horsleys to arrive in Hartlepool did so almost 150 years ago. John Horsley was born in 1848 at Wold Newton, in Yorkshire. His wife, Mary Anne Codling, was from Hinderwell, in North Yorkshire, and her father was a farmer. They married in Hartlepool in 1870. They were listed in the 1881 census as having five children aged ten, eight, six, four and two. The youngest of these was my dad's father. He was married in 1901 to Mary Allen – my Granny Horsley. She, however, didn't have roots in Yorkshire. Her father was a true cockney, born and bred in Poplar, and her mother was from Inverness, a true Scot, with the name of MacKintosh. The reason *why* they all moved here has gone with them to the grave. Maybe it was just for a fresh start, the desire to live somewhere new, right on the sea coast. But we are still here. It must be the sea air.

CHAPTER 6

THE FIRE IN
MY EYES

Sometimes it's hard to remember the past – especially if you've taken as many shots as I have! You can rack your brain for hours for a lost memory, and at other times – bang! – something from the past hits you with no warning. Music is a particularly good trigger. Who, for instance, could forget that old classic 'Kung Fu Fighting', from back in 1974? Every time I hear that song I remember my Bruce Lee period. He was big business back then, and people from all walks of life were fanatical about him. I had Bruce Lee posters plastered all over my bedroom wall, and also had a subscription to *Kung Fu Monthly*. Dad used to nark me by calling him 'Bruce Fruit'. I tried a bit of Kung Fu only to find it wasn't my game, but remained fascinated with Bruce Lee's fighting style. There were queues of fans outside the pictures every time one of his movies was on. At the end of the movie, the exiting audience would come out into the streets en masse, and start doing Bruce Lee take-offs, randomly screaming in mock Chinese, '#@/ *.!!!' Looking back on it makes me laugh at how easily influenced we all were, but still, great memories. Since his early death at the age of 32, Lee has attained legendary status. Behind the image though is a serious thinker – if anybody studies and fully understands the philosophy of Bruce Lee, they will never go far wrong.

In order to raise money to see Bruce Lee films at the pictures, Tank and I got into the coal-selling business – well, for one day anyway! Picking sea coal from the beaches was common in those days; people even had full-time jobs doing it. The tides would wash the coal up on the North Sands in a great strewn mass. We would get two coal sacks from my Uncle Keith's coal wagon, and then cycle down to the beach, where we would pick 'sea coals'. We would both sell two sacks of coal for 50p a bag, making a quid each. It was really hard work getting off the beach because the sand was so soft. We had to push the bikes because there was no room to sit with two sacks of coal dangling from the sturdy frame. The key to getting it right was the balance, as otherwise the bags would come straight off. We would return to the housing estate sweating like pigs. As soon as we shouted, 'Sea coal, 50p a bag,' they were sold straight away. It was a good idea, but for some reason we never did it again. Then again, it's lucky we didn't go into it full time, as all the coal soon disappeared when Margaret Thatcher took over. Since Thatcherism contributed to the closing of the coastal pits, the amount of sea coal deposited on the beach lessened. Beaches once full of coal wagons and merchants filling their rakings into the carts became a distant memory. Soon after the collieries closed down, and coal-fired power stations became obsolete ... doesn't that say it all?

Another song that takes me back, but for a completely different reason, is Perry Como's 'For The Good Times'. Every time I hear it I get a lump in my throat and a tear in my eye. This was the song my mam used to play just after the passing away of my hero – my dad. The death of my father totally devastated me. I am not ashamed to say that I cried and cried. As the New Year turned, his condition had deteriorated, and he had lost weight. The kidney machine had become less and less useful. In the last ten days of March, he became very ill. Mam was phoning the hospital to let them know what was happening, as they were not able to admit him without doctor's permission. My mother called a doctor out every other day in the hope that they would give permission, but no matter how much she voiced her concerns, they kept on refusing, and just told her to give Dad different drinks, some of which he was not supposed to have. In the end, the hospital sent out a card for a clinic appointment, which was the only way to get him to the hospital. When the ambulance arrived they immediately put him on oxygen – he had blacked out a few times the day before, but my mam didn't know it was through lack of oxygen. When he got to the hospital, he was put on a trolley and wheeled into see the doctor while Mam waited in the waiting room. A nurse came into the waiting room within minutes, with the news that he had died. As strange as it may seem, on the morning of his death there was a gathering of grandchildren, nieces and nephews, who had all come to see him within minutes of each other, not knowing that he was going to hospital.

I went into a shell for a year after my dad died. The 1975 FA Cup final between West Ham and Fulham took place only five weeks after his death. My cousin, Steven, came round to watch it with me, but it just wasn't the same without Dad there. I used to get scared in the house because I could feel a presence there. I didn't know at the time but it was probably just Dad saying, *Everything is alright, I'm watching over you.* One time, I went home to collect my Uncle Jimmy's giro. I opened the door, picked it up from the floor and placed it on the little box that covered the electric meter, so I could pick it up on the way out. When I returned to the front door to pick up the giro, it had vanished! I retraced my steps to find it, but I knew for certain that I'd left the giro next to the door on the little box. I know I did. No one believed me when I told them it had disappeared, but what else could I say? The giro was never cashed. About 18 months later when we moved out of the house it was found under the stairs ... unopened. Explain that one?

We went on a family visit to Derby before I could say goodbye to my mates at Rossmere. The purpose of the visit was to see my mam's stepmother, Rita. We went by train, with a big convoy: there was Mam, her brother Phillip, Aunt Ellen and her four – Tank, Kev, Ste and Kenny – and me. Philly was playing Elvis songs on a cassette player. We met an actor on the train who was in the now axed TV daytime soap *Crossroads*, who played a character called 'Carney'. He gave us all signed photos of himself. When we finally arrived, Rita, said, 'Welcome to the house that Jack built.' We all had to get bathed in front of the fire in an old tin bath, the type you used to see people using in old movies.

Derby was certainly a welcome break, and allowed us to make new friends. In Derby I started getting friendly with a good-looking girl called Angie, who lived in the next street. I fell head over heels in love with her after our first kiss. She had beautiful eyes and long brown hair. We were only 11 years old, so I guess you could call it puppy love. One day I was in Angie's house when her dad came in and said, 'If you are going to marry my daughter, you had better live in a mansion.' I just sat there speechless. Quite a lot of pressure for an 11-year-old! They say you never forget your childhood sweetheart, and Angie certainly still holds a special place in my heart. I can still vividly remember our parting, when we had a nice snog. She cried her eyes out for me. Whenever I hear the song 'Angie' by the Rolling Stones, I am reminded of her. I was lovesick when I got back home to Hartlepool. We exchanged letters for quite some time, and I went back a month later and again about eight months after that. I even had to flatten her jealous ex-boyfriend! A couple of head butts put him right. I spent the whole of my time back then with her and we had some special times together. Mam was thinking about moving there permanently and putting me in a comprehensive school called Bemrose, but in the end I wanted to stay in Hartlepool.

When I started senior school I was still suffering from the affects of my dad's death and didn't want to mix with people. I remember one morning in class when someone asked, 'Has your dad died?' I replied that he had, and did my best not to cry. I definitely couldn't be bothered with all the 'Who's the best fighter in first year?' crap and stayed well away from it all. I didn't start coming out of my shell until a year after Dad's death. But when I did, I didn't pull any punches.

There was a local public garden called the Burn Valley, which we had to walk through if we had swimming or field sports. One time I was walking through when two brothers started staring at me. I stared back.

One of them quipped, 'Who you looking at?'

I angrily snarled, 'You!' One of them started walking over to me. As soon as he was in range, I hammered him with a right hand to the chin that sent him sprawling to the ground. His brother tried to surprise me but I decked him as well, and ended up steaming into him with the boot, just for good measure.

I started courting a girl called Jill Coser who lived round the corner. She had attended the same primary school as our Tank. I always thought she was good looking, but never thought she'd fancy me. She went to my senior school, and I would stare at her when we got off at the bus stop. She would look at me and smile. I thought she was just being polite, but everyday the smiles got bigger. We ended up going out with each other for about 18 months. At Christmas I got her a necklace, just something small made of silver. When you blew at it, it would spin round and you'd see the words *I love you*. I wasn't soppy or nothing, far from it, but after all, it was Christmas. In return she bought me the latest single by Queen that I liked, called 'Somebody To Love'. Every time I hear it I am reminded of her.

I had a pal called Coto who had also lost his dad. Now and then he would break down and I would do my best to comfort him because I had been through the same thing. One night, a few of us were talking in the front room of our house when there was a big loud bang on the bedroom ceiling right above us. Everyone ran out of the house screaming, so shaken up that they wouldn't return. I had to go upstairs and check that everything was OK. There were certainly some weird things going on.

In the February of 1977, we left the house and moved into a caravan for six months. I had a fight there with a lad who was older than me. I can't remember what it was about now, but I can recall that he caught me with a couple of good punches. I always fought people older than me. My heart, determination and will to win took over as I landed some hooks to his head. Just as I was moving in to finish him, some big fat geezer – huge in fact – dragged me away to protect the other lad. As I started arguing with the fat geezer, the dirty cunt who I was just about to finish sneaked around the fat fucker and hit me with his best shot, busting my lips. I was going mad to get at him, but the big fat bastard wouldn't let me and the lad wouldn't fight back. He knew my rage would have been taken out on his face. He'd given me his best shot and it wasn't good enough. I'd get older and muscle-packed – his time would come!

Some of these scrapes would revisit me in later life. After all, what goes around comes around. Many years later I was bouncing in a pub when a bully back from the old days turned up with a few of his pals. I was buzzing and hoping there would be trouble, because I'd waited a lot of years to put this ginger bastard on his arse. My blood ran cold as I watched his every move like a hawk – if he so much as raised his voice I would be over in a shot to tear the limbs from him. I was getting high thinking of all the brutal acts I would carry out on him. Sadly though, there was no trouble that night. I followed him and his pals out of the pub and said a few nasty things to see if he would fire up and take the bait, but his bottle went and he pissed off. He must have seen the fire in my eyes. I got a little satisfaction out of it, but I still wish I could have chinned him.

I started getting back into football too. My Uncle Jimmy went to Wembley in 1976 to watch Newcastle against Manchester City in the Football League Cup Final. Newcastle had a brilliant time, even though they lost 2-1. I was brought a few souvenirs back. There was a big Newcastle flag that I put on my bedroom wall, a Cup Final programme and ticket. I was hooked and have followed Newcastle ever since. Most of the lads round our area supported Manchester United. It gave me great pleasure to laugh like fuck at them and tease them when underdogs Southampton beat them 1-0 in the FA Cup final in 1976 ... but then again, it's only a game. Losing my dad had certainly changed me, and had put things into perspective. But I was gradually coming out of my shell with the passing of time.

CHAPTER 7

CROMBIE COATS AND HAPPY DAYS

Family life changed once again when my mam married a man called Ken. She had been seeing Ken for about a year when he proposed. Mam asked me what I thought about it. Well, I had seen that Ken had put a bit of stability and security back into her life, and as long as she was happy, so was I. I did, however, make it clear to Ken that, even though he would be my mother's husband, he could never be a father to me. He understood my strong loyalty to my dad, and was happy with that. They married in May 1977, on a lovely day. Plenty of friends and family turned out. Photos are another great record of the past, and in the wedding pictures you can see quite clearly that the 1970s were in full swing. I've got shoulder-length hair and am wearing a white 'Fred Perry' jumper with a pair of blue bell-bottoms. My mate Tommy is featured, as is Jill Coser, who I had been going out with for about a year. I don't really know what happened between us, I suppose we just drifted about, as you do. Things were also changing at the older end of the family. I went to see Granny Horsley after the wedding for what turned out to be the last time. She had gone senile and died a year later.

In many ways I was revisiting the past even back then, as the Teddy Boy movement, which had been a 1950s phenomenon, came back with a vengeance around this time. I got well into the old rock 'n' roll records, my favourite of which was one by Danny and the Juniors called 'At The Hop'. I even had a Teddy Boy coat, but I only wore it in the caravan, and ended up giving it to my mate Dean, who was proper over the moon with it. Much of the Teddy Boy revival was down to the American teatime soap *Happy Days*. Everyone wanted to be The Fonz. People were selling their karate gear, relics from the Bruce Lee days, to buy new leather jackets and hair gel. There was a café near the town centre that used to be frequented by all the Teds. They'd play all the old tunes on the Juke box, 'Shakin' All Over', etc. The Teds wanted the owners of the place to change its name to 'Al's', which was the name of the diner in *Happy Days*, but they weren't successful. I reckon the owners knew it was just another fad that would pass, no different from the Bruce Lee phenomenon a few years before.

Being The Fonz was one thing, but in my heart there was only one King: Elvis Presley. Around this time the news broke that he had died. I was no different from the millions of other fans, and was devastated by his death. I went to my bedroom to mourn and shed a tear for him. It began to seem like all those I held dear were popping their clogs! The media frenzy was relentless: it was all over the newspapers, television and radio. Everyone was talking about it. Then again, some people think he is still with us. I suppose you could say, The King is dead, long live the King!

As everything was changing around me, I started developing new habits too. One day in the caravan, my mother noticed a square box in my pocket, and enquired, 'Are those cigarettes in your pocket?' I didn't answer, but she made me get them out. She grinned and told me to light one up. You probably know what tactic she was employing. But I was a dab hand at smoking. My lungs might as well have been fitted with vacuum pumps ... I was that good. As I lit up and puffed away, she immediately realised that I wasn't a virgin smoker. In fact, I had started smoking about a year earlier. I used to light her nippers up from out of the ashtray; they were the non-tipped ones called Woodbines. I couldn't have picked a more suitable brand for getting used to tobacco – they were fucking strong, burned the back of your throat like hell and tasted like shit! I think Mam knew she couldn't stop me from smoking, but at least she never allowed me to do it in front of her. Thankfully, I gave up the dreaded weed seven years ago and will never smoke again.

While I could kick the smoking habit, no scientist could ever invent a patch strong enough to stop me from my greatest addiction: fighting. It didn't take long for my family to discover this little habit either. I can still remember the horrified look on one of my aunty's faces when she happened to walk by one of my early victories. I was knocking the fuck out of a lad called Vic. Her face went whiter with every punch I landed. My hands were covered in blood by the time it was over.

Not long after this, rumours started circulating about a lad at school who reckoned he could do me. Soon enough I spotted him down the Burn Valley – a place quickly becoming my fighting homeland. He was with six of his followers. I walked straight up to him and yelled, 'I heard you've been calling me names and want to fight me.'

I still remember it as clear as if it were yesterday. There was snow lying on the ground. He was wearing what was called a Crombie coat and a pair of Doctor Marten boots. He loved himself. Before he could answer, I put the head straight on him. BANG!!

He was shook up and dazed, and slipped when trying to stand up in the snow. I waited until he steadied himself before unleashing a right hand, putting him flat on his arse, following it up with a smack that almost took his head off. It was all over in two shakes of a dog's tail. News of the victory went around the school, focusing on the ease with which I dealt out the beating. Without even seeking it, I was now the 'hardest in the year'.

Not that it was all plain sailing. I still had to learn to control my aggression – if you can't do that as a fighter, you're nothing. One incident that I am particularly ashamed of involved a family of sisters from Norway who were staying on our caravan site. I did have some good laughs with them, but one day one of them pushed me too far. I hit her. As soon as I lashed out I regretted it. It's a lesson well learned. Even though the girl recognised it was her fault, I should never have hit her. She laughed about it years later when I bumped into her in a nightclub, and pointed out the crooked teeth from where I had hit her. Still, I don't see it as a laughing matter, but it happened, and you can only put it down to experience.

The same thing happened with a mate of mine called Jimmy, who also lived on the caravan site. He was a few months older than me. Jimmy and I had some good times together. His mother had a broad Scottish accent that was hard to understand. I can remember the time he chinned a lass as if it were yesterday. She was a tall bird, about 6ft 2in, with long ginger hair. They were having an argument and then smack! Jimmy clanged her right on the button. She went down like a baby giraffe trying to find its legs. We kept in touch after we had moved from the site down to the town. A few years later, he was riding a motorbike and hit a patch of oil on the road. He skidded and went straight into a lamp post. He died a couple of days later in hospital. I was gutted. I went to his funeral but it took ages for it to sink in. Despite the incident with the Welsh girl, I have some very fond memories of Jimmy. Rest in peace, my friend.

Gradually I was realising that there was a world of fighting outside of the Burn Valley when I started getting into boxing after watching a fighter called Dave 'Boy' Green on TV's *Sports Night*. I think it was 1976. He hailed from the Fens, and was a true warrior. I loved Dave's all-action, non-stop style. Every fight he had was exciting to watch. He was a real crowd pleaser and he made a big impression on me. I used to listen to all his fights on the radio and then watch the recording on the television, as back then you didn't have 'Pay to View' TV. He was my first real boxing idol. A couple of years later, I plucked up the courage to write to him and received a reply, along with a signed photo. I was over the moon – I still have the picture in a frame.

Unfortunately I lived miles away from any of the local amateur boxing gyms, so couldn't go as regularly as I would have liked. This wasn't a major problem, as there were plenty of sparring partners to be had, such as Tank's cousin, Buller. We had a little trouble over something and he threw a boot at me, hitting me in the head. That meant game on. As we squared up, I threw an accurately painful left hook straight into his gut, taking the wind out of his sails. I hammered a right on to his chin, and it was game over – the flowers were in the post!

Other people's fights offered another opportunity to learn my trade. A friend of mine called Corbo was once having a scrap with a lad who, I thought, had a bit too much for him. A fair-sized crowd had gathered. Corbo was doing OK and was giving as good as he got, until the lad started scraping his face off the wall. The crowd cringed – Corbo's face was getting really messed up. Now that wasn't right, so I lashed out at him with a pair of Dublin boots. I almost took his fucking head off. Needless to say the fight was over, but Corbo's face was a disaster. He looked like an advert for acid peeler. I'm sure it would have been a different story if the other lad hadn't cheated.

Looking back on all these incidents, I guess you can only say that boys will be boys. I suppose the art to success is knowing what you can and can't get away with. I was certainly pushing my luck at school. One incident in particular sticks out. It was during a science lesson, when a few of us were larking around with the Bunsen burners. We had found that you could use then as water guns if you put the tube over the tap. Well, for some trivial reason the science teacher had come down the room to tick one of us off. As he started walking back up the classroom, one of the lads put the tube over the tap and another turned it on full. Water started squirting out and, at the exact same time, I picked up the Bunsen burner and directed it towards the science teacher, splashing the water all over his bald head. I tried unsuccessfully to hide the makeshift water gun before he turned around, but the sight of him with rivulets of water cascading down his face had us all in hysterics – it was just too funny.

He stormed down the classroom, looking straight at me. Gulp! He grabbed a hold of me, and started shouting and wagging his finger in my face. I managed to extract myself from his iron grip by pushing him away. But he went to grab me a second time. This time I pushed him away harder and told him loud and clear to 'FUCK OFF!'

When I swore at him all the class went 'EEEEEEEEEEE' in unison. I barged out of the classroom with the teacher in hot pursuit, and started wrestling with him as he tried to drag me to the headmaster's office. As we got to the stairs I made a break for it, pushing him down them before sprinting off. I ran out of the school and into the Burn Valley. I staged it so I didn't get home too early, but with each step to the front door my butterflies got stronger. I was certain I was going to get busted.

As it happens, though, nothing was said. Luckily we didn't have a telephone, and the school never sent a letter. I stayed away from school for about six weeks because I thought that I would have been expelled anyway. When I went back my form tutor informed me that the headmaster wanted to see me in his office. He asked me for my version of the Bunsen-burner fiasco, but as I started telling him he began interrupting me, giving the version that he had been told by the teacher. He fumed, 'So then you told Mr so and so (I'll keep his name anonymous) to "fuck off".' As soon as he said *fuck off*, I started laughing, as it sounded so funny coming from him. This was not a good idea as he went ape shit. Fortunately though he resisted suspending or expelling me, and offered me another chance. I can only think that the teacher had kept his mouth shut about being pushed down the stairs as then the Head would have had no option but to kick me out. I guess the old baldy was too embarrassed to talk about it! After all, it didn't take much to get a suspension. For instance, Corbo was suspended just for shouting at a teacher during a cricket match. It was Teachers v Prefects. A teacher called Nutall went into bat, and Corbo belted out, 'Nutall, go and fuck off and play with your nuts.' Pretty fucking hilarious. If you have ever read the 1970s *Skinhead* series of books, well ... Corbo was the absolute double of the lad on the front cover of *Skinhead Escapes*.

Even though I avoided suspension, I still got six of the best with the cane from the headmaster. I got three on each hand. But you couldn't let out any emotion, no matter how much it hurt; you just had to be brave and keep it all inside. This was repeated when I went back for my first science lesson, to make an example to the other kids. I became a bit of a celebrity, so to speak. Even so, given the choice between the cane and suspension, I would have taken the suspension any day. I had the misfortune of being caned in every year in senior school: first, second, third, fourth and fifth. No wonder I got to prefer giving beatings to receiving them.

CHAPTER 8

THE SMELL OF BLOOD, SWEAT & GREASED LIGHTNING

I first appeared in court at the age of 13. Also featured in the dock were four of my mates: Gam, Corbo, Coto and Vaughnie. It had all started from the best intentions, as we had initially decided to earn some extra money by going potato picking. We walked a good few miles to get to the farmer's field, but couldn't find any 'tatty' pickers. The place was deserted, except for a great big haystack, which in our adolescent imaginations began to resemble a bouncy castle. We jumped on top, bouncing around for about an hour, leaving the stack a wreck. One of the lads then set the haystack on fire and all the smoke from it alerted the farmer and god knows who else and all of a sudden, both he and his farm hands turned up from nowhere. We made a run for it but got caught. Well, we got taken to the local police station and were subjected to a round of interviews. We got bailed – no pun intended – and had to go back the following week to see if we were going to be charged. As it turned out, the farmer was a local magistrate and wouldn't settle out of court. Just our fucking luck! We were charged with criminal damage. We started laughing like madmen when they called out our middle names in court, provoking the judge to give us a proper roasting – verbal, that is, not the sort of roasting that footballers give to their groupies! We had to pay damages of £6 each and were given a conditional discharge for a year.

Some people say the best place for little scallywags is the boxing gym. Well, there were no gyms near us, but we improvised and started our own in an old school building. The rat-a-tat of bags, skipping ropes spinning around at blinding speeds, the smell of blood, sweat and liniment oil ... I don't know how the others used to feel, but I just loved it. We all used to get stuck in. The lads had a different impression of me after we'd traded punches because there was always blood spilt – there are no hiding places in the ring, after all. And we were intently trying to knock each other out! We were never taught how to do this and do that, we just used to fight and pick things up naturally. I had instinctive ability, and think I would have gone a long way in the legitimate boxing game if someone had grabbed me then and taught me some ring craft. You certainly couldn't fault our dedication, as we were there three nights a week for about six months.

I was a glutton for punishment, and started going to a proper boxing gym. I ended up going alone as none of the other lads were up for it. There were some good boxers there who I used to spar with. Admittedly I took some pastings, but it's all part of the learning process – as they say, no pain, no gain. I tried to learn a lot from guys like the Foreman twins, who were both southpaws and smooth operators. Ken had the best jab I've ever seen – he could snap it into your face quicker than an elastic band. It banged off my nose quite a few times. Other fighters relied more on power, like Big Ronnie, who was as tough as they come. Every time I got out of the ring after a session with him, I'd be banged up with a busted nose or a black eye, but I loved it. He was a good middleweight, and ended up fighting the likes of Herol 'Bomber' Graham in the amateur game. The main thing I learned was how to soak up the punches. An excellent junior there called Mickey M once caught me with a peach of a left hook, right on the bell at the end of the first. Everything drained out of my legs. I had to go another couple of rounds, but I got to the end. Some so-called tough guys think they can just turn up and start pasting all the boxers, but as soon as they get a beating in the ring, they change their minds. You don't see them turn up again.

The bottom line is that boxing is a skilful sport,

fought by tough people. When lads used to be bust up, the main trainer, Duncan, used to repeat his favourite saying with a smirk on his face: 'That's what it's all about.' He would even turn a blind eye to the odd bit of cheating, so long as it reflected a desire to win. There was one big guy there who used to try to bully you in the ring, using his southpaw stance to the optimum advantage. The first time we sparred I couldn't land anything on him. I thought, Fuck this, and waited for him to come in close before releasing a cracking right hand into his balls. That sapped the energy right out of him. In the end, I could take anything he threw at me, replying to each shot with interest.

My love affair with watching the professional game continued. In 1978, I started collecting all the weekly boxing supplements run in one of the newspapers. I especially loved Rocky Marciano and the Brown Bomber, Joe Louis, who is thought by many in the know to be the best heavyweight of all time. For Christmas I got the *Encyclopaedia of Boxing*, which had all the world champs in at every weight, with great in-depth action and brilliant photos. I was also given an 8mm film projector and screen, with which I could watch some of the classic fights on film. They were silent and in black and white, but when the lights went out and the film was rolling, it was magical: Marciano v Walcott, Marciano v Louis, Ali v Frazier and plenty more. Unbeatable. All the lads from school would come round to watch them too. I still have them to this day.

I passed my medical to box and was lined up to fight in the December of 1978. But some things just aren't meant to be, and the fight had to be pulled when I started to suffer with pains in my legs and heels. I was diagnosed as having 'Osgood-Schlatters' disease, which basically meant that I was growing too quickly, causing inflammation of the bone where the thigh muscles attach to the lower leg. I was not allowed to do any physical exercise for a good while. I had to wear bandages around my knees for six months, as well as having my boot heel built up by a quarter of an inch. As soon as there was a bit of wear on them, I had to get them redone. It was a good job flared trousers were in at the time, as otherwise my bandages would have shown through. If drainpipes were in, I'd have been well fucked!

The 1970s were still in full swing, and I loved all the partying. In the summer of 1978, Mam, Ken, Corbo and I went on holiday to Butlins for a week. Corbo and I were at the disco every day. There was a punk rocker there with a Mohican hairstyle. One night, after the disco, he got on the diving board in the outdoor swimming pool and dived in with all his clothes on. Everyone used to think he was mad. Happy days. I can still recall all the lasses crying at the last disco of our stay, as they were saying their goodbyes to their brief holiday loves. We would laugh at them and say, 'Look at them, daft bastards.' We certainly weren't a sentimental bunch.

I continued my partying back home at the disco night, which was held every Thursday at the local youth club. You'd see lads on the dance floor showing off or trying to act dead cool, all in order to pull the birds. At the beginning The Fonz was still all the rage, and people would turn up dressed up like him, or with T-shirts with 'The Fonz' written on them. Then disco started taking over, with the release of the films *Saturday Night Fever* and *Grease*. I have to admit that I went to see *Grease* at the local ABC Cinema with a few of my mates – you'd be surprised at how many so-called 'hard' lads were in the queue. There were two brothers called the Barnstable twins who used to go to dancing classes, and would have the dance floor cleared for them just so they could strut their stuff with two girls to the song 'Greased Lightning'. The twins were done up like John Travolta's character and the two bewers – that is, women – were dolled up like Olivia Newton John. They used to think they were film stars, but I just thought they were a pair of fucking prats.

And how could I afford all this partying? Well, I had started going to football practice with a lad from my class, who lived above a pub. On the days that we weren't at practice, he would take shots at me. With his fists. I used to let him sock me in the jaw for 10p a punch. He used to absolutely love it, he really did. I used to get £1 a day from him and he thought it was worth every penny. After all, in 1978, £1 a day was good money.

Violence didn't scare me half as much as ghosts. Sometime during the summer, I started camping out in our Roy's front garden, or slept on the couch in the living room. Roy was my mam's brother and was married to Jean. They had two kids together plus they also looked after Roy's five kids from his first marriage. Quite a brood! One night I was sleeping downstairs, when I suddenly woke up with a start. I could feel something behind me, but was frozen with fear and couldn't turn around. I tried to ignore it, but just couldn't. It was like a vibrating current of electricity. The hair on my body was stood on end. There was something in the room.

I plucked up the courage to turn around and have a look. Nothing could prepare me for what I saw. Sat down in the chair opposite was an old woman. She raised her head to look at me. I shouted with fear and leaped of the couch like a scolded cat.

I ran through the kitchen, into the passage, up the stairs, and started banging doors. I barged into Roy and Jean's bedroom, white as a fucking sheet. Roy and Jean woke up and wondered what was going on. I told them I had just seen a ghost in the front room and that there was no way I was going back down there. The look on my face should have said it all. Roy went down to check and found nothing. He said it was my imagination. But I know what I saw and, believe me, it was a ghost. A real spirit! I never slept down there ever again.

CHAPTER 9

MAKE MY DAY, PUNK

Disco stayed around for a while, but I started growing out of it when Punk hit the scene. One of my mates had bought the album *Never Mind The Bollocks, Here's The Sex Pistols*. I would go round and listen to it with him. We loved the Sex Pistols, who were notorious not only for their subversive songs, but for that appearance they made on live television, where they hurled a load of swear words at the host of the show.

When my mate dyed his hair, we all laughed and took the piss but, to give him credit, he didn't give a fuck. And that was what punk was all about. One night at the disco, my mate went up on the dance floor and started doing what was called the 'pogo'. I don't think I need explain what that one was all about. Everyone used to laugh at him because he was the first one to do it, but soon enough it became all the rage. It wasn't long before even yours truly dyed his hair. Along with my hair colour, my company also changed, and I started knocking about with a different crowd, with a rougher edge. A couple of the lads, Measor and Waller, had both just been released from detention centre. I knew them from school, before they had served time in Her Majesty's establishment for naughty boys. We often went to each other's houses to listen to any new singles or albums by The Clash, Sham69, X-Ray Spex, Sex Pistols, Angelic Upstarts, and so on. We bought guitars and a microphone so we could start our own band. Measor obtained a set of drums, using a loan from a bloke called Ken.

Punk wasn't just about music. It was about fashion too. We would wear T-shirts with obscenities scrawled on them; coats and trousers were ripped to bits and held together with safety pins and the odd zip. Measor and I wore a padlock and chain around our necks, just like Sid Vicious. I threw mine away though after an incident outside the youth club. Measor was having a fight when his opponent grabbed hold of his chain and started trying to choke him with it. The fight was soon broken up, but still, fuck that, I thought, I don't won't to be a fashion victim, and never wore one again.

If punk was about anything, it was being different to everyone else. I went to a hairdressers called 'The Knut House' and got a skinhead-style haircut, and I then had coloured blond hair with red question marks dyed into it. I was over the moon with the finished result, as it was completely different to what anybody else had. I didn't half get some funny looks from people. I had it like that for about a month. I wish I'd had my photo taken so I could show people it now and have a laugh about it.

Just like the rockers and the mods a generation before, the punks were firm enemies with the bikers. We started going to a youth club that was full of bikers, all of whom were older than us, all in their early twenties. They fucking hated us and we loved it. We introduced punk up there. The DJ started playing a couple of punk records for us, which we would dance the pogo to. Inevitably we'd get drinks chucked over us, resulting in a fight, which would always escalate out of control. There were some enormous fucking bikers, I can tell you, but we always gave a good account of ourselves.

I started seeing one of the biker's girlfriends on the side. Although she wanted to keep it quiet, it wasn't long before he found out about it. He came looking for me one Saturday afternoon with a couple of gorillas. I was with Measor, and they spotted us walking back from the town. They expected me to bolt off, but instead I started walking towards them, fucking up for it. He was taken aback when he saw that I didn't give a toss about him and his mates. He asked if I wanted to fight, so I calmly responded that I did. As we scouted for

71

a place to scrap, I looked at one of his mates, whom I knew was a right handy fucker, and nodded down at his Dublin boots. I cheekily said to him, 'I suppose I'll be getting a taste of them, will I?' He went off on one, wanting to start it there and then, but it was too busy. We eventually found a bit of wasteland, which is now the site for a doctors' surgery and health centre – ironic, I'm sure you would agree.

I slowly took my denim jacket off, carefully undoing each button as I looked deep into his eyes to let him know that I couldn't give two fucks about him. I handed it to Measor, and squared up with the girl's boyfriend. As soon as he was in range, I snapped his head back with a savage left jab. I wanted to keep him at arm's length to have a look at him and see what he was all about. I wanted this fucker to know that he had made a grave mistake in challenging me, so kept snapping the jabs home, making his eyes water like sprinklers. He changed tack, and leaped at me like a lame bear, in a desperate effort to turn the fight into a wrestling match, but I sidestepped, cracking him once more on the nose. When he recovered, I could smell his fear. He tried once more to take me to the ground, but that just allowed me the opportunity to catch him again. He had been beaten and, what's more, I hadn't thrown a single right hand.

Some old ladies who had walked past had alerted a policeman, who then came running over. The other lads bolted, leaving just my beaten opponent and me. The copper gave us both a warning, and asked for our names and addresses. He also asked our ages. I replied that I was fourteen. The biker couldn't fucking believe it. When he was asked the same question, he reluctantly answered, 'I'm nineteen.' He then said, 'If I knew you were only fourteen, I wouldn't have fought you.' I was tempted to reply, you shouldn't have fought me anyway, as I was always going to kick your arse.

Fights also broke out between punks. I remember one punk disco where there was quite a bit of barging on the dance floor. As the music got louder, the barging turned to elbowing, and so on. Nothing happened in the end, but at the same disco the following week, we decided to change tack. As soon as the barging resumed, we started fighting, even though we were as outnumbered as Davy Crocket and the boys at the Alamo. Everybody piled out into the street. One of our boys, called Tone, had the foresight to run back to the van we had come up in, and picked up a length of thick chain. He wrapped it round a good few heads, which started making things more even. But just as we were getting on top, the police arrived. They halted the fighting immediately. During the trouble one of the tyres on the van had been pierced. The cops told us to change the tyre and to fuck off immediately or we'd get banged up. We didn't stand there arguing with that and did exactly what they said. They mustn't have wanted the paperwork.

Looking back on that period, I'm amazed we didn't

end up getting banged up. We continued our escapades one night after meeting a couple of girls. Measor, Charlie and I all went back to one of the girl's houses, sneaking in through the front door while the parents were watching TV downstairs, before proceeding upstairs to her bedroom. Measor jumps into her bed, I grab hold of the other one, and Charlie starts to amuse himself. The bed began to bang against the wall as soon as Measor started to get his work rate up. In the interests of the group I had to put a stop to my shenanigans, and hold down the bed to soften the noise. Soon enough though, the door opens, and in walks the girl's dad, fucking fuming. He starts punching the walls, shouting his head off. Charlie jumped under the bed to hide, while me and Measor bolted it down the stairs and out of the house. What a fucking performance! Amazingly, Charlie was never discovered, and sneaked out the house a couple of hours later.

Punk, sadly, wasn't to continue for long, but it was a fucking great time while it lasted. After all the scrapes I'd been through, I don't know how I'm still here in one piece. My attitude to school, though, had permanently changed. One day in class, I said to the lads, 'I'm sick of this, I think I'll fuck off.' The lads dared me to prove my words, so I just pushed the table away and walked out. The teacher was shouting, 'Horsley, where do you think you're going? Horsley, get back here.' But I just ignored him and kept walking. I had a fellow comrade in hating

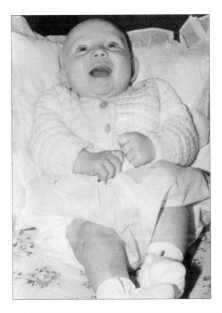

Above left: All smiles as a tiny baby.

Above right: With our dog Mickey in 1965 – according to Mam, we were inseparable.

Below: The Horsley family, with Granny Horsley in the middle.

More treasures from the family album …

Above: My mam, Brenda and her sister, Ellen, with their father.

Below left: My Christening day in 1964.

Below right: Mam and Dad taking a walk in Seaton Carew in 1964.

Above: Carefree days with some of my cousins. At the back are Susan and Graham and in the front row are Brian, Sandra and me. *Inset*: My Granda, Sonny 'Kid' Morris, an ex-boxer.

Below left: Biker babies. With Dad and my cousin Sandra.

Below right: A kiss for Mam from her little boy. Mam's friend Annie Bobbin is on the right.

Above left: My first win. Poochie is on the deck – the future fighter at four years old.

Above right: Messing around with cousin Kev.

Below: Mam and Ken's wedding. If you look hard you can see me at the back, in the middle.

Above: We are the champions! Rossmere School League winners, 1974 –
I was the goalie and I'm at the back, fifth from the right.

Below: Lanky teenagers, we three. Kev, me and our Kenny.

Dear Richard

I am pleased to hear you have taken up boxing it is a great sport. The biggest tip I can give you is train hard and be dedicated + then the actual fighting is alot easier, also use your brains and think about what you are doing don't just go into the ring + fight.

An encouraging letter written to me by Alan Minter, former World Middleweight Boxing Champion.

Inset: 17 years old, Light Heavyweight.

to have a special diet, just eat good food + plenty of it, as long as you are training hard you need plenty of energy so don't worry about it.

You sound a big lad + you are still growing, I should think in the future you will be a light-heavy or heavyweight so work at it,

Best wishes.

Alan Minter

My lovely sisters – their smiles could light up a room. *Above*: Jacqueline fooling around and, *below*, Debra.

Inset: Me and Johnny Newton back in the eighties.

Above: If yer name's not down … with Stilks, regarded as one of the best bouncers in the country – he once minded Sid Vicious of the Sex Pistols.

Below: This is the man to see if computer games are your thing – my pal Gary has a whole shopful!

school called Roger. We started nicking off lessons
together, especially in the last year. We would go to the
arcades all day or in the shops and cafés spending
money. Roger used to get money from somewhere,
although he never revealed his source to me. Once we
went into a men's tailors and bought two trilby hats –
they were fucking beauties. They came to thirty-odd
quid, which Roger settled. If I ever wanted anything, he
would buy me it. But still, Roger was my mate if he had
money or not – it made no difference to me.

He was a good fighter too, second only to me at
school. One day he turned up covered in cuts and
bruises after a fight outside – you guessed it – the local
youth club. He had been firmly on top when the lad's
mates waded in. At that time he was only one grade
away from a black belt in karate, but ended up packing
it all in. I encouraged him to go back, and went with
him. We did it for a few months, but I'm not frightened
to admit that I wasn't too clever with my legs. I used to
challenge him to Kung Fu fights in the back street, no
hands, just kicking. We would go at it, hurting each
other with full-blooded kicks, fighting for about thirty
minutes at a time. We would put each other on the
deck, but each of us would always get up, and start
going at it harder than ever. Every time we ended up
with bust noses and cut lips, but we would always
shake hands after it as if nothing had happened.

Eventually the bunking from school caught up with

us, when one day a man from the school board knocked at the door. To my mam's amazement, he said I hadn't been at school for two months! Mam tried to catch me out when I got home by asking me if I had had fun at school. I replied that it had been OK. When she mentioned the man from the school board though, I just started laughing. I had nearly left anyway so it made no difference to me. Hence my surprise when the final examinations came out and I discovered that I had miraculously got three GCSEs. Fuck knows how that happened – in one exam, for instance, I only wrote my name on the exam sheet and passed the rest of the time with a book on Bruce Lee. In spite of that unlikely success, I can only conclude that I was never really a school person. They say they're the best days of your life, but on leaving the school I felt more akin with Alice Cooper's sense of joy when he screamed out: 'School's Out Forever'.

CHAPTER 10

TRADING BLOWS, TOE-TO-TOE

I left school at the age of 15 and got my first job with a local builder who used to do houses up. All he really wanted was a young dogsbody who he didn't have to pay much. I never liked it. The builder expected you to know what you were doing straight away and the hours were long. I was only in the first week when he told me I wasn't what he was looking for. The feeling was mutual – he was a fucking arrogant wanker. If I were a bit older, I'd have chinned him for sure. I then started working on Sea Defence, at Middleton Beach, for five days a week. It was run by a government scheme which paid £23.50 a week, although I only received £19.50 a week until I was 16 as Mam took £4 a week as child allowance. The work was laboriously hard, but it went some way to building my strength up. The labour involved wire cages called 'gabions' which had to be filled up with rocks and bricks and stacked beside each other along the beach. You gradually built them on top of each other, until there were about eight or nine levels.

The hard graft complemented my return to the boxing gym. I worked with two gaffers called Denny and Bill, who would tell tales about the old days. They used to call me 'Rocky'. After eight hours of that, everyone went home to put their feet up, but I would go on to the gym to put myself through more punishment. I'd do an hour-and-a-half session: shadow boxing, stretching, skipping, sparring, pad work, medicine ball, sit-ups, press-ups. I was as fit as a lop in those days. The main trainer at the gym, Duncan White, encouraged me with my training. The other lads were getting better and better, which made sparring sessions all the more intense. One time I went a couple of rounds with a very good amateur, who had just returned from an excellent third-round win in Norway. As the bell was rung I went straight for him, jab, jab, one, two, left hook, right hand – I was really up for it. I think he was shocked at my intensity. He came back at me just as hard and we could have fought in a telephone booth. Neither of us would give an inch as we traded full-blooded shots, toe to toe and head and body. After two rounds Duncan shouted, 'That's enough or you'll kill each other.' We were both bloodied up, the sign of a proper session.

I'd come through the ordeal and satisfied myself that

I did have some real fighting spirit inside me. I decided to give boxing a proper shot, and agreed to my first fight, but that had to be cancelled when I had a bike accident. I was getting a lift off my mate Tony, and as we were belting along my foot got stuck in the spokes, throwing both of us flying over the handlebars. When I landed my teeth went through my lip, which was pretty fucking painful. Nevertheless, I was allowed to box on a show less than a week later. My lips were still swollen, but Duncan had been told the doctor was going to pass me in advance. The doctor gave me a wink, and then said with a smile, 'What's that, a cold sore.'

I sheepishly said, 'Yes.'

I may have spoken like a sheep, but I fought like a lion and won on points.

This victory impressed the three coaches at the gym, Duncan, Norman and Ernie. Sometimes an old bloke called Frank Pybus would turn up and I would love listening to his stories about the old-time fighters. He was a former boxer and later became a referee. The old veteran had a vast amount of knowledge and a good memory. I bet he could have written a brilliant book of his memoirs but, sadly, he died a while back and all his stories went to the grave with him.

If boxing teaches you anything, it is to be humble about your abilities. I remember one time when an army boy came to our gym to train for about a week. He was jollying himself up something rotten. I watched him spar and he'd go at it hard, trying to be the guv'nor, always trying to prove a point. I got in with him one session and he came at me like a steam train. Bang, bang, bang. He didn't pull his punches, he would really let fly with them. Then I noticed if I jabbed him to the body he would parry it, which left his jaw exposed. I backed him into a corner and feigned a couple of jabs into the body. His left hand came down to block my jab and in, the blink of an eye, I threw a pile driver of a right hand, which exploded off his jaw. His eyes rolled back as he went sprawling to the canvas, knocked out in the corner of the ring. He took a little time to bring round to the land of the living. Norman gave me a bit of a telling-off in private and said he could see what was going to happen. But it did teach the kid an important lesson.

My boxing successes continued when I reached the quarter-finals of the National (NABC) Championships. I was drawn with a finalist from the year before. I had the upper hand until a clash of heads in the last round. I looked down on the canvas, thinking someone had thrown water in the ring, but it was my blood. I had got cut. The ref took one look at me and stopped the fight. The lad went on to win the title. I, however, went to hospital to have six stitches put in my left eyebrow. I still trained but didn't spar because my eyebrow needed time to heal.

The night before my big quarter final fight, I should have been tucked up in bed early but, as I'm sure you've guessed, I wasn't. Far from it, actually. Instead, I went to the engagement party of a lad I worked with called Skiddy, at a club called the Wagga. I'd known Skiddy since I was about seven and all of the lads from work were going, so I thought I'd only have a couple of sharp ones and then go home. I was full of good intentions, but once I'd got a few pints down my neck and got into the party spirit, all thoughts of the big fight the following day were put on the back burner. I ended up having a skinful and the rest, as they say, is history.

I eventually returned to the ring after having my eyebrow tested in a hard fight with a lad from Newton Aycliffe. I won a unanimous decision and had a beautiful black eye the next day.

After a couple more wins, I made the North East Counties Final (Junior ABAs). I was up against the best junior light heavyweight in the country and the previous year's champion, Gary Crawford, who'd won five national titles already. Crawford was very tall at 6ft 3in and a very big puncher. He backed me on to the ropes and hit me with a big right, following it with a left and right combination of power-packed punches, which all landed flush on my chin. He put everything into them. He gave me a very strange look when I was still stood in front of him, saying, 'why haven't you gone down?' He forced me back on the ropes and caught me in the throat with a big right; the ref jumped in and stopped the fight. I couldn't swallow for days after. I later found out that I was the only person who had boxed him in the championships that year, as everyone else had pulled out and refused steadfastly to box him. Eventually, he turned pro and boxed under the name Crawford Ashley. He won the British and Commonwealth titles, a Lonsdale Belt outright, and a European title. Another tall lad I fought was from Darlington, who was 6ft 4in. He had very long arms, making it hard to get past his reach.

One of the lads in our gym, called Duane, later went on to become a well-known street fighter, who was feared and respected. We also had a young lad called Andy Tucker who later won the Junior ABA title at middleweight and captained Young England against the USA. Philly B and I used to have some proper brain-damaging wars with every punch aiming to be the last; plenty of claret was always guaranteed. I turned up one Monday and Duncan asked me, 'Will you fight Glenn McCrory on Thursday?' McCrory's people had been on the dog and bone to Duncan the night before and asked if I was available for Thursday. I'd boxed on the same show as Glenn a couple of times in the Junior ABAs. One of the lads from the gym thought I had the beating of him but I said, 'No.' For a start I hadn't trained for months. The fight was also to take place on McCrory's own club show. At the end of the day, boxing is a sport and, no matter how hard you are, it's not worth doing if the conditions aren't right.

I did, however, have to start training hard for the championships (NABC), which were only two weeks away. I was in at light heavyweight. All the boys rallied around each other for their fights. We had one lad called Carl, who fought at light welterweight, and was the best gym fighter I had ever seen. He was mixed race with great boxing ability and silky smooth skills. Because he wore white shorts with a black stripe he looked like Muhammad. I thought he would go on to bigger and better things, but he never turned pro. He could hit you three times before you landed a punch. He fought twice that day in the championships and his hands came up like puddings. The second fight was a carbon copy of the first; both fights were wars and he dropped both fighters in the last round to win each by decisions. My head was pounding from shouting for him.

The lad I fought, Eddie Ellwood, went on to become a professional bodybuilder, who made history by winning the 'Mr Universe' title five times in a row. As we started trading punches, I got caught with a couple of slicing uppercuts, delivered with accuracy to my head. The ref gave me a standing count. We carried on trading blows, until I changed tack and got him in a clinch. He was in trouble and blowing like a whale, trying to catch his breath. He'd nearly shot his bolt and I was sure I would stop him. I just missed with an inaccurate left hook, which would have taken his head off. He rallied off another volley of punches, but I overcame the challenges. Then for some bizarre reason the ref shouted, 'Stop boxing,' and stopped the fight. I told him that I wasn't hurt, but he waved me away, giving no explanation for his decision. When I told Duncan I'd had enough, he said, 'Don't get disheartened, I'll get you a return on a club show.' I was going to fight Eddie again, but when he arrived he said he wasn't fighting. This was an anti-climax for me, and I decided to finish boxing for good. Eddie and I did become good friends though.

As my interest in boxing began to wane, I began to go out more and more socially. Mod culture was on its way back in – there were Vesper scooters flying about all over, everyone was wearing parkas with union jacks on, and the group Madness were getting big, supported by other bands like Ska, The Specials, The Selector and Bad Manners. I didn't get into this scene as much as with punk: the only mod thing I ever wore was a pair of two-tone trousers. I preferred to wear a donkey jacket or an Arrington, jeans and Doctor Marten boots, and kept my skinhead hairdo. We had some great fun at discos and house parties. There was always someone who couldn't handle their drink who would end up spewing their guts up. I have a long list of mates from back then: Johnny, Decker, Peo, Piggy, Gaffo, Anth, Pod, Taller, Richie, Tesh, Finn, Micky Peart, Trav and loads more.

I hung around especially with Micky Peart. We had some good laughs. He was loud, whereas I was quiet. We'd go drinking in this rough place called the Cobble

Bar. You had to go down a set of steps because it was in a basement. The regulars would eye us up with suspicion. They all smoked dope, which was provided by a big, scary-looking dealer. He would pull out a big bag with different-sized and different-prised lumps of dope in full view of everyone. People would be in and out of the pub all night buying dope from him. No one said anything as they were scared of him, but years later it so happened that I had a fight with him. I done the cunt no problem. It turned out that the dirty rat was a police informer. So much for criminal justice, eh?

We started getting up to new and more daring escapades. One night me and two mates, Gaffo and Kev, went into a local kebab shop after a long night on the piss. After ordering three doner kebabs we realised that none of us had any money left to pay for them. As soon as they put the kebabs on the counter, we grabbed them and ran like fuck. As we were running, we heard shouting behind us. It was a geezer from the kebab shop chasing after us with a big machete in his hand! Luckily, we got away. Talk about Ali Baba and the three thieves.

It wasn't long before I started making the local papers. One night I had been drinking down the town with Mickey and some other lads, when some coppers came up to the car we were in and start looking at my jacket. I had forgotten that I was tooled up that night, and that people could see something sticking through my coat – someone must have called the police thinking I was carrying a gun or something. I was charged with carrying an offensive weapon – a truncheon – and received a fine of £50. The following appeared in the local paper:

TRUNCHEON YOUTH IS FINED £50

A youth carried a home-made truncheon in case of attack but it proved an unwise precaution for it led to him being fined £50 for possessing an offensive weapon when he appeared before Hartlepool magistrates yesterday. Richard Stephen Horsley (17) of Dalton Street, Hartlepool, admitted possessing an offensive weapon in Mulgrave Road, Hartlepool, on November 21, 1981.

Sergeant John Ness, prosecuting, said that at 11.30 pm on Nov. 21, police officers acting on a tip-off saw a Hillman car with four youths inside parked outside a takeaway. As they approached, the defendant, who was sitting in the back seat, ducked out of sight. The officers asked them to get out of the car and discovered a black wooden home-made truncheon concealed beneath the rear seat. The defendant initially denied the truncheon belonged to him, but later said he carried it for his own protection and would use it if there was trouble. Mr Michael White, defending, said the truncheon had been made by Horsley's grandfather when Kung Fu first became popular in Britain. It had not been made for a 'Sinister Purpose'. Horsley could not justify carrying the truncheon and had not been in any danger. There was no risk of him using it aggressively.

This little episode failed to temper my wild side. One Saturday afternoon, I was back in the Cobble Bar with Mickey P, just having a few pints. As I was in the toilet, I started hearing a commotion coming from the bar. When I went back in it was all smashed to bits. It only took five minutes and the bar, the optics, the jukebox, the table and chairs and all the glasses were smashed to bits. Hartlepool were playing Sheffield United and the Sheffield fans had charged into the boozer and wrecked it. No one got a kicking – they were just intent on smashing the place up and left.

The following Monday I was back in court for an assault that had happened four months earlier. Yet again, I made another appearance in the local rag:

EXCHANGE OF WORDS LED TO ASSAULT BY YOUTH
An exchange of words between two sets of youths quickly developed into a case of assault, Hartlepool magistrates heard yesterday. Richard Stephen Horsley (17) of

Dalton Street, Hartlepool, admitted a charge of assault occasioning actual bodily harm when he appeared before the court. The magistrates heard that the offence related to November 26 last year. Horsley and two friends were walking along Grange Road when they passed two youths walking in the opposite direction. Words were exchanged between the two groups, which eventually spilled over to violence. Horsley punched one of the youths who was left with a cut lip and bruised face. Mr Barry Gray, defending, said it was a 'most unfortunate and disgusting episode'. He said Horsley thought the youth he assaulted had wanted to fight him. 'The words "come on" were spoken by the unfortunate victim and I do not know whether he wanted a fight, but it was taken that way. This wasn't a mugging or unprovoked attack, it was something which came out of words exchanged," said Mr Gray. The Magistrates remanded Horsley to Low Newton for a week while social enquiry reports were drawn up.

This time I didn't have boxing to put a stop to my antics. I just wasn't interested any more, as I was busy having a good time out on the piss. I still had to serve my week in prison though. While I was in Low Newton, I spotted Collo, the lad who had stuck up for me back in the day at primary school, but he never recognised me, so I didn't say anything to him. When I told the fellow prisoners that I was from Hartlepool, they would immediately think that I was in for football violence, as there had been a lot of fighting at Hartlepool games around that time. Even though it was only a small town, with a population of about 90,000, it had more than its fair share of hard men.

I had recently been dating a lass called Joanne for a couple of months. I got on well with her dad, Jim, and we'd talk until the early hours before I made my way home. He was a really nice bloke and we got on great. I'd get invited round for Sunday dinner and there'd be a load of us sitting around the table: Joanne's dad Jim, Mam, Pat, brothers Paul and Graham, Joanne and her sister Ursula, and me. They welcomed me with open arms and made me feel a part of their family. My mam and our Sandra (the daughter of me stepsister Helen) came to see me in prison, bringing cakes and sweets, as you did at that time. One time they brought Joanne with them. As they were leaving, Joanne whispered in my ear, 'I've missed my period.' I still remember that moment vividly, when it dawned on me that there was a chance I could soon be a father.

The court day arrived and I was in the cells at the police station. As usual they were full and they put me in with this big fucker called Jimmy, a proper Jack the lad. A few years after that, I bumped into him at a nightclub, just after I knocked out one of his mates. He came up to me and stared cockily at me. I stuck the nut on him and set about him with my widow makers – my hands – laying him out cold. He was a mess and the ambulance came and took him to hospital where he stayed for about a week. As soon as I walked into the courtroom, I looked around and saw friendly faces: my mam, our Sandra, Joanne and her dad Jim, Gibbo and a few others. The jury went out to reach their verdict. It felt like ages till they came back. I had a brilliant Social Inquiry report that swayed it for me. The judge said that before my report was read, I was getting six months but because I had such a good report I deserved another chance. I was ordered to do 180 hours of community work. I was relieved.

By this time, Joanne found out that she was definitely pregnant. I was quite chuffed that I was going to be a dad. I started doing my community service. The office where everyone from the area had to meet was through in Middlesbrough. I'd get on at the town centre and used to see Eddie Ellwood on the bus going to work at Head Wrightsons. I'd sit next to him and we'd chat for ten minutes before he got off. At community service, everyone was split into groups with different supervisors. One week you'd be chopping trees at Helmsley Forest, the next week you would be painting the windows of a community centre or digging gardens over at Eston, a wide range of things.

Things at home started going badly. Mam's husband Ken had old-fashioned views, and didn't like me staying out all night. One night when my mate Coto stayed round we accidentally left all the lights on all night – it was the straw that broke the camel's back. When he got home from work the next day, Ken went mad, and we had a big argument in the kitchen. I ripped off my shirt and threw it down, wanting to fight him. My mam jumped in to stop me because she knew I'd have ripped his head off and torn the limbs from him. He told me to get out of his house, so I started shouting, 'Stick your fucking house up your fucking arse! I'll never set foot in this fucking house ever again,' and all that.

I left and went to live with Joanne's parents, Pat and Jim. I felt a bit homesick for a couple of weeks but settled in nicely. I slept in the bedroom with Paul and Graham. They had bunk beds and put a camp bed in for me. Paul would take turns with me and sleep in the camp bed and I'd get in the bunk. Joanne and Ursula were in another bedroom and Pat and Jim in the other. They had a video on which we would watch the latest films at night – it was like being at the pictures. I had some great times there and felt more like a son than a prospective son-in-law. Paul and Graham were more like brothers.

Funnily enough it was a film that got me back into boxing. One night, Paul and I went up our Roy's to watch a boxing film that had been pirated; it was a great copy and an excellent film. After, Paul chuffed, 'That's the best boxing film I've ever seen.' The film was *Rocky 3*, laughable now, but back then it was the best thing since sliced bread. We went back up a couple of nights later and watched it again. I went to the pro gym to see if I could do a bit of training there and got the OK. I went back to the amateur gym the next day, just around the time of my 18th birthday.

I was as rusty as hell. I only just managed to win my first fight back against a 34-year-old bloke. I upped the pace in the last round to catch the eye. I got a taste of snot in my mouth and I felt like spewing because it was my opponent's. That spurred me on and I hit him with a roundhouse right hand over the top, and then landed cleanly with few good short and snappy shots, turning his legs into elastic. He went down. He was one punch away from being stopped when the bell rang. I got the decision but I knew that my reactions were not fully there. I was arranged to fight a lad from the same club in a couple of weeks. He was a good fighter, in his mid-twenties, strong and fit with shoulders like a hod carrier. I knew he would cause me some problems so I went to the pro gym and sparred with Phil Gibson, who had helped George Feeney prepare for his epic title win. George had stopped Ray Cattouse in the 14th round in the 1982 fight of the year. I'd known Phil a few years. He was out of the Jake LaMotta mould and was never stopped as a pro. He was in my face all the time, making me fight every second of every round, and never took a backward step. I was made to work out angles and to be mentally on my guard; it was just the preparation I needed.

The fight day finally loomed. During the first round, the left side of my face started going numb because of how hard he was hitting me. As I sat on the stool at the end of the first, my eye suddenly closed and then opened again – it was really weird. A few years, later Harry Carpenter described in amazement the same thing happening to Sylvester Mittee when his eye swelled up and went straight back down like a flat tyre in front of his eyes. I knew I had lost the first round, so did my best to win the second. It was hard, the punches were struck with deadly accuracy and thrown with such venom, but I had a big heart and kept going forward to trade blows with him. It came down to whoever won the last round. This was high-octane, bloody and gritty stuff. We were both hugely confident; both sensed victory and fought to a standstill. About twenty seconds from the end of the fight, I put everything into a short, sweeping right hand. It was a stunning shot, which landed in spectacular fashion on the chin of my victim, who went down like a lead balloon.

Amazingly, he got up and took the count and the ref waved us to box on! Everyone was cheering. I won on a majority decision. The full show was videoed for the Owton Manor Social Club, in Hartlepool. I have never been able to get hold of the video, but I know a couple of people who have seen it. No one seems to know where it is, but someone must have it somewhere. If that person happens to be you, come and see me about it.

CHAPTER 11

LION HEART

I will never forget the feeling of being a father for the first time. I think I was more nervous than Joanne as we went into the hospital just after her waters had broken. Six hours later, she gave birth and the midwife cheered, 'It's a girl.' When I held her in my arms, I couldn't believe how beautiful she was. I was so proud. Having Jill Louise was better than winning the lottery. As Joanne's house was too small for a baby, we applied to the council, who soon came around to assess us. Luckily we were offered a house within a few days, and after taking a look around we decided to have it. After a few weeks of wallpapering, painting, getting carpets laid and so on, we moved in. I was very happy playing the father role; I changed the nappies and sometimes bathed her, as well as taking her out in the pram for walks and all the rest of it.

We lived over the road from my friend George Feeney, who was the British Lightweight Boxing Champion. I started going with him to the pro gym, only to train though, and to enjoy the crack with the lads. I would help George out with his training, joining him every morning for some road work. George was training for a fight in Italy against the Lightweight Champion of the World, Ray 'Boom Boom' Mancini. Mancini had knocked out and killed a Korean in his last fight. He viewed the bout with George as a ten-round 'warm-up', just another non-title fight. In the end, George gave Mancini one hell of a fight and almost put him down in the eighth round with a left hook. It was so close that George only needed to win the last round for a draw. He ended up just losing on points, but as the fight went out live in the United States, George quickly got recognised as an up-and-coming world boxer. They wanted to give him a shot at the title but first he had to beat the number-one contender, an American called Howard Davis. This was no mean feat as Davis had won the gold medal at the Montreal Olympics, and was voted the best boxer of the games ahead of Sugar Ray Leonard. In the end Davis wouldn't let George near him, and boxed a beautiful fight from long range. He won the decision. All these experiences got me closer to George and his family, all of whom were lovely people. One time George came over to my house with his Lonsdale Belt, and took some photos of me wearing it. The last fight of

George's pro career was in Germany for the European Title. This time he was robbed of the decision. After all, he had decked the champion twice.

People say boxing can be a cruel game, and that was certainly the case for George. A detached retina brought George's career to a catastrophic end, which prompted him to retire while still holding the British title. I went to visit him at the Eye Infirmary in Sunderland and gave him the biography of his favourite boxer, Rocky Marciano. I regard George as never having fulfilled his destiny. There can be no doubt that he is the best boxer ever to come out of Hartlepool – and we've had some good ones over the years.

While I was enjoying my boxing training, things at home were starting to get too much for me. Joanne was so moody, which made us both unhappy. She's the moodiest person I've ever known. I felt suffocated and couldn't take any more. One day I told her I was leaving. I packed my bags, kissed my daughter goodbye and went to live at my Aunt Ellen's. My aunt's second husband, Harry, had a load of boxing videos from his mate and I would spend hours at a time watching them. Our Kevin and Kenny were still living at home so I shared a bedroom with them. I gave Kenny my red-and-white satin boxing shorts and he was over the moon – he wore them for ages and wouldn't take them off.

My family had already increased with Jill Louise, but was set to get bigger when one day Ellen showed me a picture of a girl who she said was my sister. I had always known that I had two sisters, who were the daughters of my natural mother, Violet, but I'd never met them and didn't know what they looked like. Over the next few weeks all sorts of things were going through my mind. I couldn't resist, and kept looking at the photo. What were they were like now? Did they know they had a brother? Did they look like me? I made a brave decision one night, and told Ellen that I wanted to meet my sisters, but without upsetting my mam. Ellen had a talk to my mam, who expressed how glad she was that I wanted to meet them, and got in touch with Violet, who was my natural mother.

My stomach was full of butterflies when I went to meet them. Even though we were flesh and blood it was like meeting strangers, but we seemed to get on OK. I wanted to grab hold of them and give them both a big cuddle and tell them how much it meant to me by being reunited, but I didn't know how they'd react, so never said much through shyness. My elder sister Debbie was 21 and had just given birth to her second child a couple of weeks before. The other sister was called Jackie, who was 20 and had a little boy. It was incredible that they already had partners and families of their own. I went to visit each of them on regular occasions, but I didn't want them to think I was interfering so I never went to see them as much as I'd have liked to.

One night I went to Jackie's place just before she was

going to visit Violet, our natural mother. She asked me if I'd go with her. I hesitated for a moment, but curiosity got the better of me. The whole thing was going to be a surprise. We got there and went into the front room. A smirk spread across Jackie's face as her mother whispered to her and nodded in my direction. 'Who's that?'

Jackie giggled, 'That's our Richard!'

After a couple of seconds, it sunk in who I was and she let out a yelp and ran out of the room totally embarrassed. Jackie was grinning from ear to ear. Violet came back in the room and said, 'Jacqueline, you should have phoned me and I'd have made myself look decent.' We left after making her acquaintance and having a cuppa. When Jackie smiled, she could light up a room. Our Debra also has the same qualities – both were very bonnie girls. Soon after, I went to the tattoo studio and got a love heart with two scrolls running through it with Debbie's name in one and Jackie's in the other.

They used to say that I was the lucky one in getting adopted, as they had a very rough childhood. Their mam and dad drank most nights at home and were always fighting with each other. You could guarantee that if their mam got her hair done on a Saturday morning it would be rived out by the end of the day. Their dad, Jack, was a plumber and worked for the same firm for forty years. One day, their mam just walked out on them and went to live with a bus driver who she'd been seeing on the sly for years. She left a note but no forwarding address. This all happened when Debbie was in her first year at senior school and Jackie was in her last year of junior school. After that, the dad drank heavily at home every night but still managed to get up for work every day.

I never officially met this man, Jack Dunn, my biological father, but did get to see photos of him that Debra showed me. I met my sisters for the first time in 1983, but a few years before, when I was about 15, I'm certain I encountered him in a newsagents on Raby Road. As he came in, I froze and stood staring at him. Something inside of me was saying that this was my real dad. He stared back at me for a couple of seconds – when our eyes locked, I knew that he knew I was his son. It's hard to explain, but I could see in my mind's eye what he was thinking. I looked like him facially and had exactly the same eyebrows. Even though I hadn't met my sisters yet, I did know that my real dad's name was Jack. My stomach turned over when the shopkeeper called him 'Jack' on his way out. That, though, was my only encounter with him. The only other time I saw him was on the day of his funeral when I paid my respects to him in the funeral home.

I soon moved out of our Ellen's and got myself a bedsit. Funnily enough, the owner of the place was the Greek geezer who owned the shop from which me and some mates had stolen those kebabs. I tried to repay him by going out every now and then to look for any troublemakers, putting my name over his door, so to speak. And nothing ever happened when I was there. He was a nice bloke who would give me anything I wanted to eat and drink for nothing whenever I went in. I got on well with his son, Chrissy. He ended up coming with me and my mate Waller to the tattooist to watch us get back pieces. Waller wanted a Pegasus flying through the clouds, but couldn't stand the pain, so never went back to get it finished. He has still got the outline on his back to this day. I had the head of Jesus with the cross behind it, which takes up the whole of my back. I went back for a few sittings while he finished the shading and colouring. I am still proud of the final result.

Things in my personal life, though, weren't improving. Joanne used to hover about, trying to put a guilt trip on me. She would pretend that the baby had been ill, and all the rest of it. One time she said that she had just had the emergency doctor out, but if that was the case, why was she out drinking? I hate to air my dirty laundry in public, but I wouldn't want to be branded an uncaring father. Well, things started escalating when she slapped me across the face. I told her not to do it again, but she slapped me five or six times before I said enough was enough. She received a bloody nose in the ensuing melee. I know in hindsight that I should have grabbed her arms to get her away from me, but it is very difficult to be rational in those situations.

I soon made another appearance at court when I

tripped into a shop window after a night of heavy drinking. I managed to get up and extricate myself from the mess, but was picked up by the police and charged with criminal damage. The ordered me to pay £600 compensation in court. Now, believe me, that window wasn't that fucking big, so I never paid a penny of it, and have no fucking intention of doing so. They got me back into court, where the judge asked me why I hadn't paid. When I replied that I was never going to pay it he gave me three months behind bars.

I was taken to Low Newton Prison where I stayed for a week before being transferred. It was there that I met up with my mate Cliffy, who was in for six months. When I'd see him going to work in the prison gardens on a morning, I'd shout a few things at him from my cell window and he'd laugh his head off. Six months later, he was dead after a fight outside a nightclub. He was in the wrong place at the wrong time, as they say. He got into an argument with some fella. After thumping him, he went outside and made a call. Out of nowhere, a van turned up full with weapons and a massive fight broke out. Cliffy was accidentally hit by a baseball bat. He staggered over the road and died in the gutter. It was tragic; I'd walk over hot coals if it would bring him back. The lad who got done for it was one of our old mates, but there was no way he had been involved. It was shocking. After a couple of years, he was released after an appeal, and rightly so.

I was sent to Medomsley Detention Centre to do the rest of my sentence. All detention centres were rough and horrible places, operating a regime just like an army boot camp. Everything had to be done at a hundred miles an hour. In general, prison was preferable, as the detention centres were intentionally bad to give offenders a sharp shock and put them back on the lines. Sometimes it worked, sometimes it didn't. To be employed there you had to be a pure bastard. The government eventually closed all detention centres down because they were too brutal. My first day there, a right sadistic screw screamed at me as I was walking past, 'Get a move on,' and then pushed me hard. I didn't move any faster, so he went berserk. First he started slamming me against the wall to knock the wind out of me, then he banged my head off the concrete wall a couple of times before raining some punches in on me. I just rode his punches, as they had no effect on me at all. I was as cool as a cucumber, which I think unnerved one of the screws who was watching.

I had only been in there a few days when I confronted the 'Daddy'. He may have been known as the hardest lad in the place, but now he had a challenger. Everyone could sense there was going to be a confrontation. All the Hartlepool lads were buzzing, as they had someone to look up to who would look after them. But it was hard to have a proper fight in there because you were monitored 24-7. From getting up on a morning until going to bed at night you were constantly under the watchful eye of the screws. Eventually I took my opportunity after doing some works out in the gardens, when I saw the Daddy washing his boots with a hosepipe. The screws were in sight and watching us out of the corner of their eyes. But as I got closer, I decided to go for it, and walked straight up to him and grabbed the hosepipe out of his hand. I told him to fuck off and started to clean the shit off my wellies. He tried to grab it back, but I caught him by the throat, knocked him against the wall, and told him I would rip his fucking ugly head off. Unfortunately the screws jumped in, so I never got to fulfil my pledge. He later said that he wanted to fight me, but this was all talk. The reality was there was a new kid on the block, a new Daddy – me.

One day I was waiting in the dinner queue when I started to hear growling noises from the bloke behind me. I looked up at him and politely asked, 'Who the fuck are you growling at, you stupid cunt?' I went on, 'Growl like that again and I'll rip your fucking head off, do you understand, you knob head?' He nodded in the affirmative and behaved himself. You should have seen the look on his face. Within a couple of days, and after a few arguments, the word went round that I was the best fighter in the place. I got myself a cushty job in the stores, jumping the queue to get in with no problems.

The screws would try to rule the place through fear

and violence, and on the whole succeeded. The more pain you were in, the more happy they were. One day when we were playing hockey in the gym, an orderly told us never to raise the stick above knee height. When one of the lads did this, he was promptly laid out. The intimidation continued in the showers, when the gym screw would run in screaming, 'Get out,' whilst whacking you with a stick. Once a week we had to do something that was called 'the fence', which was dreaded by all. Everyone had to run around the inside perimeter of the fence. It was two miles all the way round, but it had to be done twice straight off, making it four miles. People would be spewing up, some would cry with pain, and the ones at the back got kicked and dragged around. A few hours later, we'd be put in to teams and have to race each other. But if you weren't giving a hundred per cent, you were punished.

Even though I was glad to see the back of the place, my behaviour didn't improve after I was let out. Only a few weeks after, I went to the Lake District with Gaffo, Bob, Gibbo and Toddy. We were all pissed and singing, 'Hartlepool, Hartlepool, Hartlepool.' Not surprisingly, they wouldn't let us in the local nightclub and we gave them some frisk – that is, leg pulling. They called the police. Unfortunately Gibbo wasn't thinking straight, and he picked off one of the coppers with a cracking right. They banged us up, and gave Gibbo one hell of a kicking in the cells. He was taken to court, remanded, and given three years. They let the rest of us out after about six hours on the condition that we left town straight away.

I suppose you could say I was bloody lucky. I don't know who was looking down on me at that time, but I was living a blessed existence. Not long after this I got into a fight with a bouncer at a nightclub. I had been smoking some blow – marijuana – and started missing punches. He picked me up and threw me through the doors. Everything seemed to be happening in slow motion. Just as he started bouncing me off a couple of walls, my boxing savvy took over and, at last, I connected with a punch. He went straight on his arse, but I didn't follow up. It was the weed. I stood back and just stared at him. He pulled himself together, mumbled something and went back into the club.

Another lucky escape, considering. Not long after that I got involved in the most intense fight I had had so far. It was late at night, and I was walking past three blokes sitting on a pub wall. I was preparing myself for some sarcy comment, but decided to get mine in first. The biggest one was glaring at me and, as I was walking past, I seethed aggressively, 'Who are you looking at, you fucking doyle?'

He didn't let me down when he snarled in reply, 'Who the fuck are you calling a doyle?'

He came at me and swung a big haymaker. I ducked, but could only keep one eye on him as I was also tracking his two mates. I missed with a couple of wild swings. The doyle's mates, though, weren't moving, as they were waiting for him to finish the job. I regained my composure and focused all my attention on him. I moved in distance and landed a destructive hard-hitting right hand, smack on the button – The Muckspreader, as I like to call it. He collapsed in a heap on the deck, out for the count. His mates looked at me and never said a word. The big fella was asleep and wasn't moving – I had flattened him.

I started jogging away from the scene, looking back about every thirty seconds. The lads were bent over him and he was still stretched out. I had visions of putting the local radio station on the next day, and hearing the newscaster say that a man had been killed in a fight outside a pub. I checked the local papers, but luckily there was nothing about it, meaning he was OK. I was very thankful that I hadn't killed him.

I started seeing a girl called Gail, who was the sister of one of my mates. We ended up getting a flat together on the seafront at Seaton Carew. At night, I'd smoke a little blow and listen to Bob Marley songs or watch a bit of TV. When we got to know the couple that lived in the flat below, they said they thought that a family of Rastas had moved in when they heard reggae music being played all the time. As a result I didn't go out drinking as much. But when I did go out, I was still getting into scrapes. I went with my friend Kevin H to a nightclub where he expected some trouble with the bouncers. As it happened, it was a quiet night. There were five bouncers there, so I thought we should get them to earn their money. We piled in, just the two of us, and flattened all five of them. At that time, Kev's brother was top boy in the town, perhaps explaining why there were no repercussions.

I really enjoyed living by the sea. I started doing some jogging on the beach every morning for about thirty minutes, filling my lungs with all that fresh sea air. Unfortunately we ended up getting a council house in another part of town – Gail was pregnant and we didn't want to bring a baby up in a dingy flat. The house was too far away from our friends and family and we were never happy there, though we got on well with our neighbours, Colin and Kathy. Gail went to look at a house not far from her mother's because she heard that the couple there were looking for a swap. The exchange went through with no problems. Anyway, when I went for a look at the house I couldn't believe it. What a coincidence! It was the same house I'd lived in a couple of years earlier with Joanne. I told Gail this, but she wasn't bothered and we started preparations for the move.

Things took a turn for the worse when I was unfairly charged with theft. Now I admit I am many things, but I am certainly not a thief, and never will be. I had borrowed a friend's video card and got some films out but for some reason they were never returned. The shop called the police and I got pulled in. They had just installed a video camera and, of course, I was on it. It was sod's law that we were moving house on the same day I was due at court. To make matters worse, Gail was nine months' pregnant and due anytime.

I wanted to be in and out of court as fast as I could so I could help with the house move. I pleaded guilty to get it over and done with. I was expecting a fine, but then the judge remanded me for ten days. I was gobsmacked, speechless. It seemed to be OK to give sex perverts bail. What the fuck's it all about? Because I pleaded guilty I was convicted, meaning that I received no privileges like other remand prisoners. They put me straight into A-wing of Durham Jail, and stuck me in a cell for 23 hours a day. The day after I was remanded, Gail gave birth to a baby girl. My mam phoned the prison to relay the information, but the bastards never told me, and so I didn't find out until the eighth day when I got a letter from Gail. After the shock came the emotion and I had a little weep. I wept with joy because I had another daughter, but also with sorrow because I wasn't there to see her come into the world. The next two days went like two weeks. Finally, I was back at court and had a different judge, who shook his head when he heard I had been remanded for something so minor. I was ordered to pay £300 compensation and was released.

I went straight to the new house but there was nobody

there. I knew Gail must have been at her mam's so I went round there. There was a few people there and they all said, 'Welcome home.' Gail handed me a little bundle and said, 'Here's your daughter.' I got a shock when I saw how small she was because I had expected her to be bigger. I was a bit scared in case I squeezed her too hard because she was so delicate.

I quickly got into the routine of changing her nappies and taking her for walks. She was daddy's little girl. We used to call her 'Shitty', not through maliciousness, but because it was a pet name. Then again, seeing it written down now does make it look different. She used to think that was her name until she started school because that's all she got called! I still saw my other daughter Jill on a regular basis. Things had certainly changed a lot – not only had I increased my family, but my criminal record was bigger too.

CHAPTER 12

BLOOD TUB

Guess what? I made another return to the sweet science of boxing, putting me up there with Frank Sinatra in terms of comebacks. This time I was training with the Boys Welfare. I was there for about ten months. The training was hard: five nights a week and Sunday mornings. You had to complete the pre-training run in a certain time, otherwise you were sent out again. Training consisted of a round of skipping, followed by a round of shadow boxing, before moving on to boxing staple: press-ups, pads, sit-ups, punch bag, step-ups, sprints from wall to wall. Peter, the coach, operated the exercises in circuits. One punch-bag exercise in particular was a killer. You had to hit it with two jabs and then a ten-punch combination, no more than two seconds to get your breath back and the same again for a full round. You were fucked afterwards, but it was first-class conditioning. I soon reached the peak of my fitness – I was 13 stone, rock solid, without an ounce of fat on me.

We all did our bit for charity too. We were sponsored to do a ten-mile run to help raise money for gloves and punch bags for the club. I think my time was about one hour and fifteen minutes. We were like a big family but we trained hard and we sparred hard. I liked the feeling of raising money for worthy causes, so I did another charity run with my mate Bob. It was a nationwide event called Everybody Wants To Run The World. The pop group Tears For Fears released the record and the proceeds went to charity. Well, I did my bit.

At the Boys Welfare Club, you'd think everyone hated each other if you watched a sparring session because it was always heavy. As the big guy, everyone would try to put me on my arse: welterweights, middleweight, light heavyweights. But nobody ever floored me, although it did keep me on my toes. There were some really good fighters in the gym and some went on to win national titles. There was Biff, Kev M, Chrissy, Kev C, Graham, Ray, Stewey, Tony, Alan, Garry and others whose names I've forgotten, but they all know who they are. Once I got caught with an elbow and my eyebrow burst open like a torn pea pod. The coach, Peter, advised me to go to the hospital so they could have a look. It was sod's law that it was the same eyebrow I had had six stitches in years before. Four stitches later and I was rebuilt. This was all part of the game – if you got cut, you got cut, so what?

Hartlepool has a long boxing tradition. It all started on the beach at Seaton Carew where the fighters fought bare knuckle. In the early 1900s a boxing booth was established on the corner of Burbank Street known as the 'Blood Tub'. The Blood Tub always drew the crowds and you were guaranteed a good punch-up. Hartlepool was a booming ship port and someone would go round the docks and pick five coloured seamen for what was called an 'All In'. One man in each corner and one in the middle. When the bell rang it was every man for himself. The winner was the one left standing at the end. That was always a big crowd puller. During the depression, people fought each other for boxes of groceries. You can see why all the best boxers come from poor backgrounds – hungry fighters literally are the best.

Hartlepool had one brilliant boxer in the early 1900s called Jasper Carter. He was the Lightweight Champion of the North of England for six years. All in all, he had 300 fights, nearly all of which went over 20 rounds. One time he was matched with the then World Featherweight Champion 'Peerless' Jim Driscol. The day before the fight, though, Driscol pulled out and it was the biggest disappointment in Carter's career. Carter fought in front of 80,000 spectators at Celtic

Park, in Belfast, against the Irish Middleweight Champion, Jack Lavery. Although Lavery was a stone heavier than Carter, Carter produced the goods with a first-round knockout and stunned the massive crowd. He died aged 63. They don't make them like Jasper Carter any more, what a fighter.

I was now working for the council on a job called site clearance. There wasn't really that much to do but sit in the cabin and play cards while the supervisor waited for a phone call. We'd only get two or three calls a week – it was an easy job. I was working with a lad called Jimmy, who I knew from community service. I was also working with a lad with one arm called Davey, who unimaginatively became known as 'Davey One Arm'. Friday was payday, so at dinnertime we'd go to the bank and get our wages, have a bite to eat and go to a pub called the Grange and sink a few beers. After a few drinks, you didn't feel like going back to work so you either went back late or not at all. The gaffer was cushty and never used to say nothing as long as you never took the piss.

So I guess you could say things were going well. Of course, those are the times when you have to start thinking – what will happen next? Well, not long after, Gail told me that a lad called Bernie had been trying to tap her up. This geezer must have thought I had 'mug' written on my forehead! I happened to know him and where he drank. One night I went to find him with my mate Mark, and sure enough we found him in a nightclub with a couple of lads and lasses. I watched and waited from over the road. At this stage, I was hugely dangerous. When they came out, I walked over to him and cuffed him with a rollicking right hand that put him straight on his back and sent him beddy-byes. That's the nearest he was going to get to Gail! I put the boot into his boat race – that is, face. I remember thinking, Who's the mug now Bernie?

Davey One Arm came round to mine a few times with some wine that he used to make, which blew your fucking heads off. One morning, at about four o'clock, Gail went into labour with our second child. As we were waiting for an ambulance, Davey One Arm walked past, drunk. He came in and said, 'If it's a boy will you please call it David, after me?' I told him I'd think about it. When Gail was giving birth, there was a panic because the cord had wrapped around the baby's neck, so the forceps had to be used. It was a boy and I was over the moon. When he came out, it took a bit for him to cry. I think we nearly lost him by the look on the nurses' faces, but he soon started to cry and there was a sigh of relief all round. He had two black eyes and marks on his head off the forceps but as each day went by he began to thrive. The nurse asked, 'What are you going to call him?' I had never thought of any boy names, as I expected another girl. But for some reason, I opened my mouth and uttered 'Terrance,' and that's what we called him.

We moved house and went to the Rossmere area of town. We were near Rossmere Park and I'd take the kids there and have a stroll round and we'd feed the ducks. Terry was still a bit too young to understand, but Donna used to love it. Around this time I started tracing my adopted family again – it must have been the feeling of being a father, and wanting to sort it all out. I was one of four children that Violet had, meaning that there was another sibling to trace after Debra and Jacqueline. It turned out that I had an older brother, who had also been given up for adoption. I applied to go on the television programme *Surprise, Surprise*, hosted by Cilla Black, which would help people trace their missing relatives. I went down on the train to London with Gail. Everything was paid for. The film crew were very nice and it took a couple of takes but I got my plea right in the end. We ended the day off with a visit to Madame Tussaud's, the famous waxwork museum. It was brilliant and you'd think the dummies were going to come alive because they looked so real.

I was sent two tickets by the TV company to go back down and see the show but I never went, and watched it at home instead. Debbie and Jackie were watching as well. During the show, Cilla handed over to a bloke called Gordon Burns who was introducing a new item called 'Searchline' where viewers recorded their own pleas to find relatives and loved ones. He was telling people about the all-new 'Searchline' and how it worked and then he said, 'We start with Richard Horsley from Hartlepool,' and I came on. I can't remember exactly what I said now. I did have it on tape years ago but it was recorded over by accident. Isn't that always the way? Unfortunately though, we never found our brother. I would get pulled up for months after the programme by people saying, 'I seen you on *Surprise, Surprise*,' or asking, 'Did you find your brother?'

That, however, didn't put a stop to my search for family members. I met a lad called Stewie when doing a bit of security work, and he told me about a book he had been reading by a medium called Doris Stokes. I was so intrigued that I got it out of the library. I was fascinated by it and wanted to know more about the paranormal. I got the phone number of a well-known spiritualist and phoned her up. They called her Ruby and she held meetings every Thursday night, so I went along. At the meetings she would tell wonderful stories to a packed room. I would just sit there in the background and listen. I'd been going for about four months and the philosophy was excellent, but I wanted more. I needed proof on my own terms.

I decided to stay away for a couple of weeks. I got a photo of my dad and started talking to him in my mind. I told him that without proof I would give up on the meetings. Well, at the last meeting that I planned to attend, just before it ended, Ruby suddenly said, 'I've got a man here called Tom. Someone here knows him.' She described the kidney dialysis machine and all the tubes, how Dad had died, and other things about him, all of which were true. I couldn't open my mouth. Then she said, 'Someone here has got a photo of this man and they talk to it with their mind.' Well, that blew me away and was all the proof I needed. I never said anything but I did write Ruby a letter and told her that message was for me.

My sister Jackie had post-natal depression when she had her daughter Stacey, so I looked after the baby for a few weeks until she was a bit better. This was around the same time that I started getting back into football. I started going to Brinkburn Sports Centre with my mate Robbie once a week for a game of five-a-side. I started playing in goal for a Sunday team, although my goalkeeping record took a hiding when I let in four goals in my first game. As the weeks went by, I became more proficient and started playing on a Saturday afternoon as well. After a couple of months playing on a Saturday, Sunday and five-a-side during the week, I became a good goalkeeper. I would never duck out of a challenge and would pick up loads of bumps and bruises. I was very physical and would love diving at players' feet for the ball. One Sunday during a game, I went for a fifty-fifty ball with the opposition's attacker. I dived at his feet and won the ball, but then I heard him screaming, 'They've gone,' and he passed out. He'd had both his legs broken! The ambulance came on to the pitch and stretchered him off, as he was out of it. They called him Faccinni and he had both his legs in plaster up to his waist for months.

One morning, a letter arrived from Halifax Town FC asking me to go for a trial at their ground. When the day arrived, I got my stuff together and went by train with our Kevin. The manager was an ex-Hartlepool player called Billy Ayre. I remembered watching him play for Hartlepool in the 1970s. There was a song that all the fans would sing which went: '*He's here, he's there, he's every fucking where, Billy Ayre.*' There were loads of people at the trial and we were put into teams and played a game. A few minutes into the game, I dived at a player's feet and won the ball, but as I dived I took all the skin off the side of my leg. It was bloody painful, and I decided there and then that I would be doing no more diving. As a result I missed a couple of opportunities to win the ball. The game ended 2-2. I never got picked, but didn't expect anything as I had had a shit game. I had played for about 18 months this time. There were only a couple of games left until the end of that season. When it finished, so did I and hung up my boots for good. I've never played since.

CHAPTER 13

PREDATOR

For a few years my mam and Ken had lived in a bungalow. One day when she was cooking the tea, she asked Ken to watch the pans while she nipped to the shop around the corner. When she got back, the pans were boiling away but there was no Ken. She called out for him but there was no answer. After checking most of the rooms, she walked in the bedroom and found Ken lying on the floor unconscious. He had had a massive stroke. It caused complete paralysis down one side of his body, and as a result he needed round-the-clock care. Mam couldn't face putting him in a home so devoted her life to looking after him. Even if he could do something, he stubbornly refused to. He wanted my mam to be at his beck and call 24 hours a day.

Don't get me wrong, I've got a big heart and am a

compassionate man, but my sympathy for Ken soon wore thin. Every night when Mam put him to bed, he would pull out the catheter tube he was supposed to use, meaning that the bed sheets would be pissed right through. All night he'd be shouting to be cleaned up. He used to ask to be put on the toilet about twenty times a day, but would usually be bluffing, and would shout at Mam just as she was back in the room, 'Brenda, I'm finished, it was only wind.' He would sit in his wheelchair in front of the TV, and would empty the full bag of his piss all over the floor. He was a proper nightmare and I felt sorry for my mam. She suffered with tennis elbow through having to lift him all the time.

When I moved into Mam's house with Gail, Ken was as bad as ever. One day, when Gail and my mam were out shopping, he started moaning, wanting to be put on the toilet. I told him that it would be wind, but he insisted it wasn't. I said, 'Look, I'll put you on but I'm not getting you off, you have to stay there until my mother gets in.' He agreed, so I wheeled Ken to the toilet and put him on the pot and left him. Two minutes later, he was shouting to be off after, surprise, surprise, another false alarm. I repeated, 'You are staying on the bog until my mam comes in, so stop moaning,' and closed the door. He was sat there for an hour. The family have laughed over it a few times.

At this time, I started going to another boxing gym not far from where I lived. The trainer was Anth, the lad who had that fight with Tank all those years ago. I started going up there a few times a week to hit the bags and get a bit fitter. There was a lad in the gym called Andy Tucker who was an excellent boxer. He was in two National finals in the middleweight division, NABC, which he lost on points, and the Junior ABA, which he won. He was robbed in the quarter-finals of the European Championships against an Italian. I had masses of respect for Andy. I started sparring with him and gave him some good work, which brought me on a bit. I enthused at my progress and started wanting to have some fights. Andy had boxed for Young England a few times and had just been chosen as their captain against Young America. He was in full training and I sparred a lot with him. One day the TV people from the regional news programme *Look North* came with their cameras to the gym to interview him and also did a little profile about the club. I had a fight lined up the next night, but my opponent never turned up because he had seen the TV programme and saw me inflicting pain on the punch bag and said, 'Fuck that, I'm not fighting him.' I met another boxer at the factory where I worked, and asked him to try and get his trainer to line me up for a few fights, but nothing ever came of it.

Anth also did some bouncing, and asked me if I fancied getting into the racket myself. I started working the doors with Anth, Brian, Peter and Rick in a very busy pub with two floors and a disco upstairs. I learned the ropes from the lads: how to be fair but firm, how to be always in control and never flustered, and how to control the crowds and queues. We had a few fights, but generally things went fine and I had some good times working with them for about four months. The song 'Footsteps' by Womack & Womack was a really big hit at the time and reminds me of that place.

I eventually managed to get a fight against a big guy, who had won seven of his eight fights. His only loss was avenged by a knockout in the return match. A load of boys from the boxing and the bouncing came down to watch me. At the show, I could see the look of concern on people's faces. Some of them asked if I was fighting the big man, concerned for my safety as he really was gigantic and towered over me. As well as these attributes, he looked a deeply terrifying man; he had an air of confidence about him, which I was determined to shatter. I wasn't going to have any sleepless nights over the size of man, as it's the size of the fight in the man and not the size of the man that matters. As the bell went, he came at me like a cannonball and tried to put me away. I took some good shots from him, a jarring left and a flinchingly painful right! I was going to have to take some of the steam out of him. I opened up with my arsenal of weaponry and we traded toe to toe. I had a burning desire in me to win and started to get him on the back foot. I was looking for that one special shot, but had to be patient. Then I put him down with the famous Horsley Muckspreader right hand … an unstoppable force. Incredibly, he got up and took the count. The ref waved us to continue.

I went after him and picked him off with a right, just like a predator. I was all over him like a rash! This guy was on a wing and a prayer when he threw a chopping right hand that whizzed past me – I was blessed it missed! I had to turn it on and step it up, because I was chicken fodder if he connected with one of those shots. I could see that his wasted efforts were tiring him. I boxed him from range and kept tying him up, swinging lefts and rights, all of them smashing into his head with an unrelenting ferocity. By now his face was covered in blood and he was about to go down when the ref stepped in and stopped it. I had won – I had defeated my Goliath.

I had my eyes set on the ABA title and was training hard for it. On the day of the ABAs, I was a little excited, as this was what I'd been waiting for. We arrived at Gateshead Leisure Centre and went to get weighed in. But the 'jobsworth' official in charge said the weighing in of boxers was over. A heated argument ensued, as he wouldn't let me step on the scales. The official said that every club had been sent a letter saying that boxers had to be weighed in by 7pm, and it was now 7.15pm. It was the first time we'd heard of such a letter but he still wouldn't let me step on the scales. My dreams of winning the ABA title ended right there, I was really devastated. Later, we found out that there was a letter, but it wasn't sent to the coach like it should have been. It had instead been sent to the social club, where the treasurer had read it and stuck it in the drawer, forgetting afterwards to tell anyone about it. When I heard this I felt like pulverising his face with my Muckspreader. What made it worse was that I really believed I would have gone all the way. A silly incident like that destroyed a man's dream. Not surprisingly, that done my canister in and I started to drift away from boxing.

Family life was more than a diversion; after all, I had three kids now (Jill, Donna and Terrance). I'd always take them out to the park, which they loved. I was a proper father and it felt great; those times are very precious to me. I wanted Jill and Terrance to grow up like brother and sister, so took Jill off Joanne's hands as much as possible. Jill was getting taller and prettier all the time; a chip off the old block.

One night, I was woken by somebody banging on the front door. It was Anth, the boxing coach. I welcomed him into the living room. I hadn't seen him for four months. He spouted out, 'Richy, I've just been talking to a bloke from Blackpool on the phone. There's a boxing show tomorrow night and they're desperate for a heavyweight. Will you fight?'

I retorted, 'Are you joking? I haven't trained for four months; I'll be blowing after thirty seconds.'

He pleaded, 'Howay, man. It'll be a night out down Blackpool.'

I made the point that I would be the one taking the punches. Anyway, maybe I'd taken too many punches round the head in the past, but somehow he talked me into it. The next day, five of us crammed into this little motor with all our gear in and headed west for Blackpool. After a three-hour journey – which seemed more like six hours – we arrived. We drove up and down the front a couple of times looking for the nightclub where the show was being held.

Outside the place there was a big banner announcing: 'LVA Boxing Championships, Tonight 7pm'. It was 6.30pm by the time we got in. The place was big, and a large crowd was expected. The atmosphere was already hot and humid. I saw the doctor and got weighed in. I was to fight the 16th fight on the bill. I remember thinking, 16th, we're gonna be here all night! The night dragged on and on, with the heat becoming unbearable. The place was jam-packed to the gunwales with between 1,500–2,000 people. I tried to have a kip but I couldn't because it was too humid. Eventually around midnight, I was told to get ready and put the gloves on. I felt physically depleted and drained of energy, and had no get up and go left in me. I wanted a bed, not a boxing ring.

I started to shadow box and there was no oomph in my punches; I was very lacklustre. Anth put the pads on and I hit them. My mam could have done better, I was terrible. I was sluggish and drained and had no power. The heat had sapped all the strength out of me. The lads

127

tried to gee me up, but to no avail. The bloke came and shouted, 'You're on.' We made our way through the crowd and the mandatory cigarette smoke to the ring. A large proportion of the crowd were the worse for wear. A few were shouting 'TYSON' at me.

We waited about five minutes and the opposition still hadn't showed; they were playing the waiting game. I decided to sit down on the stool and wait; after another five minutes they eventually showed. He was a local lad from Lancashire, and the crowd started cheering as soon as he appeared. In the first round, I tried to put him away but my punches had nothing in them – I might as well have been hitting thin air. It was then that I knew I had to really dig deep if I wanted to hear the final bell. I threw a clever little corkscrew right. A great shot, but it just didn't have the power behind it.

My opponent was about 6ft 4in tall and in good shape – he couldn't be pulled apart in the usual fashion. So I tucked my chin up and moved to the ropes to use them to fight off and draw him in. I also wanted to lean off the ropes to regain some energy. He didn't throw many jabs, preferring to release combinations. I dug deep and summoned up every bit of strength. I had to gamble, and put all my energy in one punch, to try and hit the jackpot. I threw a cracking right uppercut. It just missed the bastard! I did hit him with a clever left hook to the body in the second round, which really hurt him, but I was too tired to follow it up. In the last round I was so wiped out that for the first time in my life I tried to get disqualified. He was throwing punches non-stop. I backed to the ropes, catapulted off them and BANG! I nutted him bang on his forehead. As he turned away in pain, I hit him with a good stiff jab! The ref jumped in and gave me a severe warning and deducted a point. He was the only person in the place to miss the nut, as he was on the blind side. The crowd had seen it all, and booed me for the rest of the bout. I made it to the last bell but lost on a unanimous decision. I'm sure that I would have beaten him inside of two rounds if I had been in shape.

It wasn't long after that when I got back into bouncing, and made more good friends. I knew a pub landlord from the early days, who told his bouncing agency that he wanted me on his doors, as he knew his pub, The Clansman, would be in safe hands. This agency was called A1, and was run by two local lads, Mick Blackwood and Mick Sorby. They both said they knew my face when we met. I definitely knew Sorby's as he had a nasty reputation. He was a proper battler. Not long before I met him, he had just had a fight with another hard man called Philly B. He bit his nose off – he took no prisoners. Philly B was certainly no pushover as he was a former boxer. I got on great with Mick, and he ended up being Best Man at my eventual wedding.

My bouncing partner at the pub was called Charlie. In the best of doorman traditions, his credentials carried some clout – he'd been to prison for violence, and shoving guns down people's throats and the like. I knew him from the caravan site as a kid, and even then he was a high-profile nutcase. When Charlie worked the door, he wore a steel plate around his stomach so that if anyone hit him there they would bust their hands. We'd have a few sociable drinks and a good chinwag and everything would go all right. When gangs of unruly looking lads came in they were told in no uncertain terms that they'd better behave themselves; when you tell them like that it either goes one way or the other but most of them lose their bottle when they see that you mean every word, especially when said with fiery eyes shining at them.

But of course, there would always be a bit of trouble – why would you have bouncers if there wasn't? One night, a bloke inside the pub had a bust-up with his woman and threw a massive wobbler. He started to smash all the glasses that were stacked up waiting to be washed, destroying at least sixty in the process. Charlie was out of earshot downstairs checking on the bar, but I managed to get back to the door in time as this psycho was just about to leave. He marched straight towards me with a giant snarl on his face. I stood in the way to block him. He threw a punch at me, but I slipped under it and snapped out a straight right that landed smack on the button. This hammer of a shot immediately put him down, and the floor show was over. He was lying on the deck groaning and covered in blood. Charlie returned and picked the guy up to take him to the toilets to get cleaned up. My hand was throbbing, so I looked down. There was a whopping great gash in my knuckles, right down to the bone, and claret was pissing out – I'd only gone and whacked his front teeth out! The teeth were stuck in my hand! I still have the scar to this very day. He went to the police a couple of weeks later, after he had heard he could get compensation from the Criminal Injuries Board. I got banged up for two weeks as a result.

The kids were my life and I loved them to bits. I wanted everything to be as normal as possible for them. We had birthday parties for them both where we'd invite their school friends and relatives. My mother would always have a big spread on for them: sandwiches, cakes, pop, crisps, jelly, ice cream, a birthday cake with candles on, and there'd always be games like 'Pass the Parcel' and 'Musical Chairs'. For the adults, there would be plenty of lager. We had some great times. An old friend of my mam's called Mary always called in with sweets for the kids and our dog Cassie was always licking the salt from her feet.

Life couldn't have been better but, as sod's law would have it, things started to get bad. I had a feeling that Gail was being unfaithful and it was just a matter of time before we split up, but it was going to kill me to lose the kids, so I kept my mouth shut for their sakes.

They were doing well in school and had a happy home – I didn't want any unrest for them. But at the same time I didn't want to be played a fool. There's an old saying that I'm sure most of you will be familiar with: What's good for the goose is good for the gander. Well, I too could play that game, and it wasn't long before I started seeing a young lass who came into the pub, a bonnie girl called Angie who was only 18. Another time I went back to a lass's house when her boyfriend was out. I think her name was Jackie. I knocked on the door and within ten minutes we were in bed. She called me 'Merlin' because she said I was a wizard underneath the sheets. All of a sudden, Jackie said, 'Stop, I can hear a noise.' The boyfriend had returned and was only stood on the stairs listening to us. Talk about getting caught red-handed, I was caught red-ended! I could hear him trudge back downstairs and go into the living room. I think the only reason he never came in the bedroom was because I'd left my coat in the front room and he had a look at the size of it and thought, He's a big cunt. I put my clothes on and went downstairs. The boyfriend said, 'All right, Richy.' I sheepishly and undiplomatically said, 'All right, Johnny, I didn't know she was your bird or I wouldn't have or fucked her.' That didn't go down too well. I put my coat on and left. I didn't know his full name, I only knew him as Johnny and I'd never seen him for years. I saw her a few days later walking down Church Street with two black eyes.

I was wanted elsewhere, so I worked in loads of different pubs. I worked the roughest bars in town, all the trouble spots. On Bank Holidays I would be guaranteed at least three fights. When there was trouble, I'd be straight in to sort it. Sometimes I'd have some rough and tumble and end up chinning a few because that's the only language some people understand. I worked the doors with numerous lads: Andy, Philly, Trev, Marcel, Kenny, Eddie, Martin, Mick Sorby and many more. I had fought some tough cookies but the first real hard man I fought, called Big George, was when I was on the door. This man could fight and was in his prime, strong as an ox and about 17 stone of muscle and gristle. He'd had a grievance with the doormen of a pub one night and went off his head and knocked them all out. Then he exploded into a fit of temper and just went from pub to pub knocking bouncers out. We were called to a pub that had our doormen on. Big George had just wiped out all the bouncers; there were shirts ripped off, teeth knocked out, claret and glass everywhere. He had just left, and was heading in the direction of our pub.

I raced back before he got there and stood at the entrance with Blackie, one of the other bouncers. He turned up just at chucking-out time. You could cut the atmosphere with a knife. He had already pummelled ten bouncers. Straight away, Blackie started to fight with him, giving it his all. But then he started to take a thrashing, so I dragged the geezer off and threw him to the ground. A load of people were already in the street and plenty more were coming out the pubs. The crowd was there – I knew this was it and that I was ready.

He got up like the terminator and stood in the middle of the road and roared, 'I want to fight you, now!' I walked over and he came towards me. I moved in close and was ready for the clash. I clattered him with two sharp right uppercuts; both landed one after the other. Bang! Bang! Normally when you land an uppercut it's all over, but this man could take a hell of a shot. He was still on his feet, so I battered him with a flurry of combinations: right, left, right, right, right and a sweet right hand. He went down. For good measure, I booted him in the head before turning around and quickly walking into the pub, away from the scene. Everyone in the place was buzzing at how quick I done him. After we got everyone out, we had a lock-in. Soon enough, Big George came back and started banging on the windows, whilst waving a knife about. We wouldn't let him in so he threw a wobbler and stabbed all the tyres on the cars outside. Not long after that, we settled our differences.

Around that time, two bodybuilders that fancied themselves came in to the pub. They were whopping big blokes – and didn't they fucking know it? One of them kept weighing me up. I didn't know whether he thought he knew me from somewhere or whether he was just staring because he was cocksure of himself. I personally hadn't seen any of them before. The one who kept staring had overdone it on the sunbed because he was as brown as hell, with a David Dickinson tan. They finished their drinks and started leaving. You should have seen the walk on the pair of them, you'd think they were each carrying an invisible carpet under each arm. It looked stupid to me, as they portrayed themselves to be hard as nails. As 'Mr Sunbed' walked past, he stared at me with a smug look on his face, so I followed them both outside. I said loudly, 'Here, Chippendale.'

When he turned around I said, 'What's your fucking problem?'

He went for me, trying to grab me so he could use his strength for some rough and tumble. But I was equally fast and unleashed a furious right uppercut on to his chin. His legs went from under him like a baby deer. They say, the bigger you are, the harder you fall and, in this case, that was correct! He hit the deck like a broken lift. Mr Sunbed's mate threw his hands up and pleaded, 'I don't want nowt, mate.' Sunbed was trying to pull himself together like a pair of worn-out curtains on the floor, but he was fucked and didn't know what day of the week it was. I ordered the other one, 'Pick your mate up and fuck off,' and went back inside.

After about five minutes had passed, I went outside and they'd gone. I got a shock though when I checked my hand to see if my knuckles were swelling or had any bruising. There was false tan on my knuckles! I still chuckle about that to this day.

Every Sunday I'd travel to different spiritualist churches. It gave me spiritual enlightenment and I enjoyed getting away from the hustle and bustle of the doors. One night I was told by a medium that I had gypsy blood in me. He could see the horse-drawn trailers of my ancestors going back generations. I didn't know about my bloodline because I was adopted, so I put it to the back of my mind. I did that for two years. I often wake up during the night and most times I find it hard to go back to sleep. One night when I woke up I saw what I believe to have been the spirit of a young girl, stood at the side of my bed. She looked about eight years old, with long dark hair that went past her shoulders. She was wearing an old school uniform and a white hat, just like that worn at St Trinians, the Catholic school I used to play football against. For a couple of seconds, I was startled. She never spoke to me, but just stared. Strangely enough, I felt a nice, peaceful energy coming from her. I also sensed another spirit in the room, which I couldn't actually see. They both vanished after ten seconds. I haven't a clue who they were or what they wanted.

My boxing career may have been over, but that didn't stop me from going to the odd sparring session. I went back to the Boys Welfare for a few months. By then I was weighing in at fifteen and a half stone. I always liked it at the Welfare. It was always a challenge when I got in the ring because all the young guns I sparred with would give me their best shots. Not long after, I started going to a kick-boxing gym. Every session started with a run and I would always trail in last. I noticed they were brilliant with their kicks, but not that clever with their hands so I'd get in the ring and spar with them just using my hands, in order to bring their punching on. I'd do eight rounds straight off. The younger kids couldn't understand how they were fitter than me, but couldn't outlast me in the ring. It was all down to one word: experience. The trainer there was keen for me to have a few fights and then enter the British Championships. He said I had what it takes, but I wasn't really into all that kicking malarkey, so declined his offer.

CHAPTER 14

IT'S THE WEAK MAN WHO HOLDS BACK HIS TEARS

Things never stand still. After four years of my mother looking after him, Ken had to finally go into a home because of my mam's ill health. Her elbows were shattered through lifting him and she now had osteoporosis from all the cancer treatment she'd had in 1970, which drained her bones of calcium and made them incredibly brittle. Back then, the kind of treatment she was receiving was fairly new, and the side effects were not yet known. She even had to get an electric tin opener because she broke her wrist in two places while opening a tin with a manual opener! My own family life changed when, finally, Gail and I split up. It had been on the cards for a long time and we only stayed together because of the kids. I'd been prepared for a split for months but it doesn't matter how much you prepare yourself, when you lose your kids, it hits you harder than any physical blow. It broke my heart. A strong man cries – it's the weak man who holds back his tears, thinking it a sign of weakness. But when you don't cry, it all builds up inside you, causing breakdowns that can destroy you. You feel much better if you can cry because it releases a lot of built-up tension. I never got to see the children for about six months. In consequence of the pain of that episode, I became very wary of letting anyone get too close to me. There remains a little distance there with my kids, but I love them more than anything and have a bottomless pit of feelings for them.

I started to become friendly with a girl from Middlesbrough called Heather, a lovely lass. We went to the pictures to see the Kevin Costner film, *Dances With Wolves*. I went out round Middlesbrough with her a few times, drinking and nightclubbing. One night she came to my pub with her cousin, who I set up on a blind date with my mate Rob. We all went up to Middlesbrough for the night. I was teasing Rob saying, 'She's not up to much, but she'll do for you,' and things like that, winding him up. But when she turned up Rob was over the moon, as was she. He moved in with her for about five years and had two kids together. My relationship with Heather, though, took a turn for the worse when I passed the crabs onto her from some girl. She came in the pub loudly shouting, 'Thanks for the dose of fucking crabs.' I stayed cool and said, 'It's OK, you're quite welcome.' I never saw her again, I wonder why?

Not long after that I started working at a pub on the seafront, a karaoke bar that was always full to the brim. I was working with a lad called 'Vulture'. He was a popular bloke whose relations would come to the club, whom we would have some good nights with. One night the manager told us that the owners were getting Lee 'The Duffer' Duffy over for protection, in order to look after the club for a few weeks. For those of you not familiar with the Duffer, here's a quick history of the man:

Name: Lee Paul Duffy
Weight: 245 pounds
Height: 6ft 4in
Age: 26
Job: Taxing drug dealers!
Background: Violence!

Attempts on his life: Numerous! Shot in the knee! Shot in the foot! Petrol attack to set him on fire!

For some reason fate kept us apart, as I never ended up meeting the man, but I heard plenty about him. Lee Duffy was a man apart and someone who only comes around once in a lifetime – a total one-off. There have been a lot of things written about him in the press, but there are two sides to every story and Lee's family have never fully told us their side. They are very distrustful of the press after Lee was made out to be some kind of monster. I also think that if Lee had been born and bred in London, he would have been an icon. He was Robin Hood, Dick Turpin and Muhammad Ali all rolled into one. A good friend of mine from bouncing, Brian Cockerill, had once fought Lee. He told me that the punch Lee hit him with during a fight was the hardest he'd ever been hit – and Brian's been hit over the head and legs with hammers, axes and machetes. He said Lee was very fast for a big man and had phenomenal hand speed. He ended up doing four years for GBH – although he only served two – and was sent to no less than eighteen jails. As soon as he arrived at any of them, he would seek out the hardest man in the joint, walk straight over to them and scowl, 'I'm Lee Duffy.' Bang! Bang! Bang! They would be clattered into submission. In every jail, he became 'The Daddy'.

What is frightening is that when he died he had just turned 26 years old and was five or six years away from his prime. This was a man who would go into the local pubs of his enemies alone. He'd put a see-through bag of money on the bar and leave it there and sit in the corner. He had some bottle, or no fear. He must have done it half a dozen times and not once was the money touched, although there was always plenty of interest until they found out who it belonged to! When entering certain nightclubs, it was not uncommon for the DJ to announce to thousands of punters, 'Lee Duffy has entered the building.' He had a fierce rivalry with his counterpart on Tyneside, Viv Graham. When Lee went to visit a relation in Durham Jail, Viv was also in there having a visit from friends. Lee walked straight up to Viv's table and demanded of Viv, 'Do you know who I am?' Viv told him to fuck off, and that was the start of it all. I would have put Lee against any man, and I mean any man.

Lee was a formidable-looking giant of a man. His presence was felt before he had even entered a room. He had such a presence about him that it has been said that he could go into a nightclub with 1,000 people in the place and within 10 minutes there would only be 100 people left in the building. He would not need to hit anyone with his fists, but his presence was felt. Someone who knew Duffy described him as a schizophrenic. When he once had petrol thrown over him, he just whacked the geezer and broke his jaw before he had a chance to pull a lighter out. When he had a gun pointed at his belly, he just wrestled his opponent to the floor. He was fearless.

Duffy was supposed to come in one night to the pub, but sent a couple of naughty lads from Middlesbrough in his place. Another week later the manager said, 'Lee Duffy is coming tomorrow night.' But he never turned up because he was entertaining friends in 'Boro. Later that same night he was stabbed to death in a fight. It was

25 August 1991. He was killed at 3.30am outside the
Afro-Caribbean Centre in Marton Road, Middlesbrough.
Apparently an argument had kicked off in the centre
and the other man, fearing Duffy had a gun, swung out
with a knife. A great hard man, Lee Duffy has passed
into legend since. May he rest in peace.

I had a number of new bouncing partners after Vul got
nine months for assault: Dickie, Andy, and then Lee –
not Lee Duffy. It was usually a merry night and the only
trouble was from drunken families. One time when
there was a big row, with plenty of fighting between the
family members. One geezer faked a heart attack. The
ambulance came and he was wheeled out with an
oxygen mask on his face. Andy said to me that he didn't
think the bloke was for real and sure enough, we found
out later that he'd faked it. When I wasn't working, I
was out drinking with the lads. For some reason I picked
up this bewer – a lass – who I had known for a few years.
She had a face a bit like a bulldog chewing a wasp. She'd
also had the coil fitted, due to the size of her fanny – she
could have had wall-to-wall carpets fitted in there! The
next morning, our Tank picked me up and was shocked.
He'd known her years as well and gasped, 'What the
fuck are you doing with her? She's a whore. I'm
surprised at you. She's had more cock-ends than
weekends.' I knew that already but when you are out
every night, you just go with the flow. I was single and
if there was any loose skirt at the end of the night that

looked half decent you don't turn your nose up at it, know what I mean.?

This lass worked at a nightclub, so I would always be in there getting loads of free drink with the lads. It was a place where I had lots and lots of fights. On one occasion, I was talking to a woman when I noticed, over the other side of the room, a bloke throwing his arms about like a windmill in a threatening manner. He was shouting something but I couldn't make it out because of the noise. He was with another bloke. I realised he was shouting at me, and excused myself to the woman and made my way over to the two men. I stopped to ask my friend Buller to watch my back. The thing is, people like this can't be talked to. I wasn't going to mess around with this crazed windmill and his sidekick, Don Quixote.

I hit the mouthy crazed windmill with a thumping right, a left, and a final right, all smack on the chin. He fell apart and was out for the count before he hit the deck. I turned to Don Quixote and he went off like the Disney cartoon character Speedy Gonzales. I eventually caught him and whacked him with a right, which didn't connect properly with its target, but was still severe enough to put him down. Fear kept this loon going, and he started scrambling under the tables in this packed club to get away from me – it was like a *Carry On* film! As the bouncers arrived, I was putting the boot into the plonker without much success. He was like a bumblebee on speed!

The doormen couldn't revive the other one and after about ten minutes, the ambulance rolled up. We were on the top floor of the club and the doormen had to carry him down the stairs while he was still unconscious. They wired his jaw up at the hospital. He drank through a straw for a couple of months. He later told someone that the punch he was hit with was like being hit with a sledgehammer. It turned out he had a reputation as a fighter, and was known as the hardest man in Wingate, a tough colliery village in County Durham. I had been talking to the smaller lad's ex-girlfriend, which had started the whole thing off. Buller quipped to me afterwards, 'What did you want me to watch your back for? You were having a fucking laugh.'

What is it with boyfriends and their ex-girlfriends? Another night, I was talking to two sisters who I hadn't seen for a few years. One of their ex-boyfriends was hovering around looking for trouble. He thought I was trying to tap one of them up. He wanted a fight but, as I was enjoying my chat, I pretended to be scared of him and said, 'No.' He grew another foot taller and his chest plumed out another six inches like a rooster. I finished my drink and said my goodbyes to the sisters before going up to him. His head collided with my fist; he was dropped down a peg or two and looked no more dangerous than a spring chicken. He was destroyed, but I couldn't resist putting the boot leather in as well because he was a cheeky cunt. The bouncers came over and picked him up and threw him out of the club.

I had so many fights in this club that it started to become my own territory. Another fight that sticks out happened not long after the jaw-breaking incident. I was at the bar getting a drink when some geezer points his finger in my face and drawls, 'Don't I know you?' He was looking snake eyed at me like a typical big-screen gangster. He had a ciggie in his mouth, and thought he looked rock hard. Getting well into the scene, I drawled back, 'I don't know, but they call me Richy Horsley.' Clint Eastwood would have been proud as I then battered him with a left hook that landed with a strange dull thud. Mr Movie Gangster was stood there leaning against the bar and staring out into space – he was knocked out, but still standing up. 'Hello, is there anyone in there?' I spoke again but never got a response so I walked away and left the drink. When he came round, he went to the hospital, and I was told afterwards that his jaw was broken in two places.

I got on well with most of my fellow bouncers, except an Irish bloke, who came to the town after doing six years behind bars for a stabbing. He was about 6ft 3in. For some reason, he wanted to build himself a reputation and started playing up to me. Obviously not the brightest kid in the class. I had a quiet word with him and told him to get in the toilets if he wanted to fight me. He had a good look into my intensely piercing

eyes and realised I was serious and croaked, 'No.' I
found out he'd only been out of prison a couple of weeks
when he carved someone else up in Carlisle. He was
currently waiting to go to the Crown Court. He had
quickly married a girl he had just met to make himself
look more respectable. But the judge saw through him,
and added five years behind bars to his marriage
sentence. Couldn't have happened to a nicer fella.

I started to work at a huge place in the town centre,
which was split into two parts. There was a bar and a DJ
downstairs, and another bar and disco upstairs. We
looked after the whole shebang. I knew before I started
to work there that I would be fighting all the time, as
this place was an arena full of dude spark plugs. In my
18 months there I saw plenty of doormen come and go.
On my first night, they told me about this bloke who
comes in every week who wouldn't see his drinks off at
closing time. And sure enough, on my first night he
refused to leave. Every time he was asked to see his
drink off he'd pick it up and wave 'bye-bye' to his drink
to 'see it off'. Obviously a comedian. I walked up and
told him to finish his drink, '... or I'm taking it away
from you.' I don't like people taking the piss or liberties,
so you have to be firm with them. So when the prick
just sat there smirking at me, I reached over and grabbed
his pint and poured it over his piss-pot sized head.
Before he could move, I followed it up with a straight
right that flattened the prick out of sight. His mates

shouted that they didn't want any trouble and left immediately, taking Mr Piss Pot to the hospital, where they found out I'd broken his nose, not to mention shattering his ego. Suffice to say, he never tried his little tricks again. The man did consider pressing charges but then thought better of it.

I had a fight one time with a lad on the stairs. The lad knew me from when I was young and thought he could take me. We started going hammer and tongs at it. I was trying to get my footing so I could get some leverage, but it was awkward. You see, the problem with being tall is that your centre of gravity is that much higher, so you can be easily put down if your equilibrium is compromised. But once I landed one on him, he went down. As he was laid across the stairs I cracked a couple more into him. The doormen at the top of the stairs were shouting, 'Richy, he's had enough,' but I knew that already. You see, you had to have control as a bouncer, as there were so many cry-baby customers who would rat to the police if you so much as spilled their drink.

CHAPTER 15

CRAZY HORSE

This world is full of lunatics. I remember one New Year's Eve, when I'd been working since noon and had a few drinks and a few fights throughout the day. I was still with the lass from the nightclub. I was somewhat pissed by the time we got to her brother's house, where the lass's 13-year-old daughter was sleeping. As I was going to the bog there was a commotion on the landing. Some cockney lad was trying to get into the bedroom where the young girl was. I went out and clipped him about the ear before staggering back to the toilet while he was escorted downstairs. Then all hell broke loose when the lad's pal, Big Bri Suckling, one of our locals, started screaming that he wanted me in the garden. Now I didn't want to fight him as I was properly pissed, but what can you do? Big Bri was a first-class lunatic who had the strength of an ox. People were frightened to death of him. His nickname was 'The Caveman' because he is the closest thing you'll see to a caveman in the 21st Century – a man with no fear and unnatural strength!

As soon as I got in the garden, BANG! He rocked me with a cracking right. My drunken legs turned to jelly and I went down. I didn't know where the fuck I was. He jumped on top of me and started letting the punches go. They were smashing into my face with sickening thuds, but I couldn't feel any pain as I was so pissed. Everybody was watching, but nobody dared say anything or intervene. While I was being beaten to within an inch of my life, the cockney lad booted me in the head about five times. I remember thinking, I wish I were sober. I thought Big Bri was going to kill me because he kept smashing away. I was telling myself to stay with it. After what seemed an eternity, he got off and it ended.

I managed, somehow, to get up from the ground and I ran at Big Bri and tore into him with empty punches. People watching jumped in and pulled me away and convinced Big Bri to leave. The only reason he stopped laying into me had been because he thought I was dead. I nearly was. He had a couple of rings on and I was cut to ribbons, the flesh on my nose was cut wide open and my eyes were both sliced open above and beneath. I was in a proper state. I couldn't see out of one eye, so two days later I went to the Eye Infirmary and they said the eyeball was grazed where the pupil was, but it would heal. I stayed away from bouncing until I healed up. Soon it was all over the town that I was done easy and there was a new kid on the block – Big Bri. He revelled in the glory and, time after time, told the story of the fight. It was all pats on the back and free drinks for the new King.

The prelude to my rematch with Big Bri took place a few months after the beating. I received a phone call telling me the cockney lad was in a certain nightclub. I went straight down and got a pint. One of the doormen let me stand on the fire-exit back stairs. He told the cockney he wanted a word because he believed he'd been smoking dope. The door opened and the cockney was led through like a lamb to the slaughter. He swaggered in and the bouncer shut the door. Come into my web, the spider said to the fly! I dropped my pint in a flash, but as I went for him I slipped in it, and I fell down the stairs! Somehow, I managed to grab hold of him, taking him with me. I just don't seem to have any luck when I'm around stairways and spilled booze! I let him have it to head and body. The cunt was squealing like a pig. I left him outside the fire doors at the back of the club, laid in a heap!

One down, one to go. Next in line: King Kong. It was time to fight Big Bri! He'd had his 15 minutes of fame and glory, but if he wanted to keep my title he was going to have to kill me. I went to the club where he was hanging about. I had my back-up team with me in case of any foul play: Ryao, Vul, Eric and Mick. I didn't go in but I looked through the windows and saw the big twat in there with his back to me. The butterflies started fluttering in my stomach. Doubt started creeping into me: was it the drink or was he the better man? I had to find out. I waited over the road. He came out and bellowed, 'So you want another good hiding, do yah?' He was very cocksure of himself. He came at me and threw a big right, but he was too slow and I managed to block it. I put a couple of big jabs on him and he went down like the *Titanic*.

Now it's my turn, you cunt. I jumped on top of him and started smashing him to bits. The sustained punching broke both my hands. I'd given my all and made a real mess of Big Bri; he was making funny gurgling noises and was choking on his own blood. I thought I had killed him. The ambulance arrived pretty sharpish and he was rushed to hospital; it was touch and go for a while, as he was at death's door, but luckily he pulled through.

I was back on top. My new name, 'Crazy Horse', stuck after that little episode. That's when the whole thing exploded. Word spread like wildfire and soon every loon within fifty miles was heading my way for a scrap. I got locked up a few times but I always had witnesses, and so I was never charged. Even when I just wanted a quiet night out, trouble always found me. One Sunday night I was out with the lass from the nightclub. We went to a place I used to work a few years before. There were two blokes at the bar, who I had to gently push aside to get the drinks. One of them grimaced and snarled, 'Who the fuck are you pushing?' I bit my tongue and ignored him. Then he threatened, 'Do you want chew?' Chew means trouble. When I said that I didn't, he blasted, 'You better not, if you know what's good for you!' I got the drinks and went to the other side of the room, but I couldn't keep the stupid twat out of my head. He kept glaring over at me and saying something to his pals. I resigned myself to the fact that a quiet night was now out of the question. I weighed up the situation; there were three of them and one of me. The odds weren't fair – I pitied them! After what seemed like an eternity, the trio of agitators decided to leave. I stood in front of the door and blocked their way, confronting them head on.

The prick with all the mouth was wondering what was going on. 'I do want chew,' I said. And then, BANG! My big right-hander lifted him out of today and into tomorrow. The wanker didn't know what had hit him. Loyalty wasn't something his mates subscribed to, as they quickly said they didn't want none. They had turned an ugly shade of white and shit themselves an even uglier shade of brown. Some woman started screaming her head off. The manager told me to leave before the ambulance arrived, which I promptly did. Now you would think that would be an end of it, but the bloke I had hit started saying that I had used a glass ashtray on him. Why he couldn't tell the truth, God only knows. I went to this pub one day to sort some trouble out, but the lad I wanted to see had pissed off but, funnily enough, there sat in the corner with a group of mates was the cunt with all the mouth. It was like walking into a lion's den. As I went outside and started walking away, I heard, 'Oi, you!' I turned round: he's standing there with a load of his mates behind him for back-up. He shouted, 'Who do you think you are? Don't ever come here to sort chew out in my pub.' I could handle three easy, but this was a little different. For one, there were women present and I didn't fancy spilling any blood and hearing a shrill shriek again – the last one hurt my ears!

I ignored him – there were too many of them. I wasn't going to give them the chance to massacre me; I'd had enough when I was drunk at the hands of Big Bri to go through it again! Instead I used my brain, and went straight over to my mate Eddie's boozer. As luck would have it, there were a few of the lads in there up for a scrap. We jumped in a couple of motors and went over to the bar I had just left. I stormed in to find the fucking prick sat down on his ownsomes. His pals must have known I'd be back and fucked off – they'd deserted a sinking ship and he was the only rat left on it. He steadfastly refused to come into the car park to fight because my friends were there. As he started to raise his voice I thought, Fuck this. I gave it to him. I shattered three of his ribs with a single body punch, with which he suffered internal bleeding. He was an ugly bastard anyway, but after what I threw at him, he could take the lead role in the next Hammer House of Horrors movie. The barman told me later that when the ambulance carted him off, he thought the geezer was dead.

Needless to say, the ugly cunt never came back for more in person, but he did hire an underworld hard man to do me over for two grand. The bloke he hired was twenty stone and as strong as a bull elephant. Word quickly spread all over the town. Everything was set for a certain night. As I went to the nightclub with the lads, you could feel the electric in the air. I was in one room, the hired hand was in the other. The head doorman was begging me not to fight in there but I told him to fuck off and he walked away with his tail between his legs. I had a couple of drinks as steadiers and fumed, 'It's time.' But when we went in the room a lad I knew said, 'He's just left, he's bottled it at the last minute.' That was a big comedown because I'd been psyching myself up all night for him. A few weeks later, I spotted him in the nightclub and stood eyeballing him, but he just shook his head as if to say no and turned away from me. You don't get much for two grand these days, do you?

The lass from the nightclub made enough trouble for me to deal with. I was like a clockwork automaton, all you had to do was put the key in me, wind me up and press the 'go' button. There was one local geezer, a well-respected hard man, who started tapping her up in the nightclub. This bloke, called Davo, fought bare knuckle and had beaten some very good men; to my knowledge, he had never lost. He was rumoured to have gypsy blood in him. He certainly looked the part, as he was shady skinned, had jet-black shoulder-length hair, which he sometimes wore in a ponytail, wore a bit of gold, and had the mandatory tattoos. Nobody wanted chew with him. When the lass I was with threatened to tell me about him trying to tap her, he had brusquely replied, 'What can Richy do with me? He can do nowt with me. I'll beat him easy.' When I was told about this, I was incensed and stewed with it for a week. Luckily enough, Davo and his pals walked into a pub I was working one Saturday afternoon. I took the afternoon off because I wanted to get the job done right away.

I went back with Vul and Andy. It wasn't a secret that there was going to be trouble. Some people were sitting in prime spots, waiting for the action. At this stage I had reached a rock-solid, muscle-packed sixteen-and-a-half stone, and was 6ft 1in tall. I was wearing an England shell suit, I had a skinhead haircut and stubble on my chin – don't laugh at the shell suit, they were all the rage then! I said to Vulture, 'I'll wait until he goes to the bar and go over and offer him outside.' But Vul advised, 'Nah, just get stuck in as soon as you see him.' I was toying what to do when he walked in behind a load of his mates.

I went straight over. He read the right hand I threw at

him, and tried to slip under it, but he was too slow. BANG! The pile driver connected with him. He crashed to the deck; I must have caught him with a good one because there was plenty of claret all over him. As he was lying there, dazed, and looking up at me, I bent over him and whispered, 'Stop messing with my woman.' Then I hit him with a peach of a left hook on the side of the jaw. His eyes rolled and he went out like a light. He had lost a few teeth and had wet himself into the next century. I stared up at his mates, but none of them would look me in the face. I shouted, 'Come on then, who wants it?' Silence. I walked out the back door and jumped in a motor. After that, the customary ambulance turned up and took Davo away.

That's when the lies started to begin. I hit him from behind, I used an ashtray, I ran to the cops for protection afterwards, all that shit. Why do people make up lies like that? Since Davo had such an impressive reputation, people believed the lies. It was talked about all over town and the place was buzzing. Davo started thinking of revenge. He went into training for eight weeks to prepare for the second fight. People started betting money on the outcome. But before I could take him out, I had to deal with all the little arseholes he sent my way.

There was a friend of Davo's called Philly, who used to run the doors in the town. He was a bit of a tough guy, and was also well connected. He was at least 25 stone, as big as they come, but a fat fucker overall. Well, one night we saw him in the nightclub, pumped up with Dutch courage. He started being a total arsehole, but I ignored him. The next week, he did exactly the same thing only with more front, so I thought, I've had enough of this. I shouted, 'Oi, fat cunt! You're getting on my fucking tits.' He slammed his drink down and came straight for me like a charging hippo – he wanted blood. As soon as he got near me I weighed into him with a mighty right hand and a head-jolting left hook. I broke both my hands as they landed – the cunt's huge head was as hard as a brick wall. He went down in front of the bar on the tiled floor. BANG! The fat bastard shattered both his knees, what with the weight of him. Despite the pain from my hands, I was driven on to keep punching his fat head; I found his squeals with each hit gratifying. A couple more and he was knocked out. The doormen wouldn't come near me, but the manageress of the club was on my back screaming like a banshee. She thought she had a death on her hands. Fatso went to hospital with two broken knees, a broken jaw and got stitched up like a football.

So why couldn't things be left at that? The cunt tried it on, he lost, end of story, you would think. But no, it wasn't long before the truth of the tale was distorted. Now I had taken him out with two other lads. Of course, one was a Kung Fu expert, and the other smashed his legs up with an iron bar. I just finished him off like a coward. What a fucking fairytale! So more bad publicity went round the town about me. To keep the matter open, Hippo man and his family got in touch with one of the hardest men money could buy, Viv Graham. But they only told him the cock-and-bull story.

Let me introduce you to Viv Graham's pocket history:

Weight: 252 pounds
Height: 5ft 11in
Age: 34
Job: Pub & Club Protection
Background: Boxing
Attempts on life: Two! Shot at outside nightclub!
Restaurant gun attack!

Viv Graham was a hard man with a heart of gold. He took every fight with a pinch of salt. His size and boxing skills made him an excellent insurance policy against the thugs and drug dealers who polluted the pub and club scene. His promising boxing career had been cut short by a 'frozen shoulder'. After Viv impressed the local under boss by beating up a big-time gangster, he was quickly catapulted to the next level – Newcastle City Centre. Some say he changed from a man who wanted to make pubs and clubs safer for everyone into a bully who struck fear into the very hearts of the very people whom he was supposed to protect. Some mobsters enlisted the help of a heavy to eliminate Viv in a winner takes all bare-knuckle fight, but the plan failed when Viv didn't show after being warned of an ambush.

It wasn't long before I heard from the man. Someone pulled up as I was working the door of a club and said, 'I've had Viv Graham on the phone asking me about you, he wanted to know what happened with Philly.'

I asked, 'What did you tell him?'

He answered, 'I told him the truth and also told him you were a nice bloke who wouldn't take a liberty.'

Viv went on to say to my friend that he had a feeling the hippo wasn't telling the truth and left it at that. One thing is for sure: if Viv did come looking for me, what a fight we would have had. It had all the makings of a classic. Sadly, Viv was shot dead outside the Queens Head pub on New Year's Eve 1993. As he lay dying on the pavement, he asked his friend, Terry Scott, to lift him to his feet.

'I can't let them see me like this,' Viv said.

It was a pleasure to have received respect from such a man.

I still had two broken hands from the hippo-man beating. After hearing that Viv wasn't getting involved, I was beginning to think that the matter was closed, but then a couple of dykes I'd known for years came up to me in the club. One of them said, 'I hear you're fighting Davo again, aren't you frightened?' I spat out, 'Am I fuck, he's the one who's getting knocked out, not me.' Well, it turned out that some blokes had approached

Davo about having me gunned down. Fair play to Davo though, as he said he didn't want anything to do with it, and would sort me out on his terms, not on anybody else's. After I found out about this meeting, I was very aware of potential traps. A geezer who I barely knew was torturing my ears for me to go to this pub one night for a lock-in. He must have thought I was born yesterday. I found out later that Davo and all my other enemies were in there, and this cheeky cunt tried to deliver me on a silver platter. My pal Mick Sorby saw him in a pub afterwards and knocked him cold with one punch. There was a stench in the air because the geezer had shit himself, and I mean literally shit himself. Come in, brown, you're coming through!

CHAPTER 16

BOYS TO MEN

Things were getting too hectic in town, and I needed a break from all the chew. Luckily I landed a job installing heavy electric cables in Port Glasgow. I went up, strangely enough, with a lad I had knocked out some years before, called Bernie. We became good friends. On the way there, the radio in the van was playing the Number One hit record 'End of the Road' by Boys II Men – they must have played it three times before we got there. We finished that job in seven days, and were then sent to a job at Wallsend in Newcastle. Overall, a very welcome break.

It didn't take long, though, for the trouble to return. I received a phone call on the morning of bonfire night from – guess who? – Davo. He was ready to fight. I told him I'd been out all night, and asked him to call back later, at teatime, which he duly did. He wanted to fight straight away, but I said he would have to wait until seven. We arranged to fight in a nearby car park. My mate Andy drove me over. Sure enough, on arriving, I spotted Davo, as well as a couple of his relatives dotted about to relay news of the fight back to people. I got out of the car and went over. We shook hands and he said, 'I've got to fight you, Richy, it was a bit fast the last time.' He was trained up for this and looked impressive in a white vest. I took my coat off and we squared up. We were stood there and he was waiting for me to make the first move. I threw a light feeler punch to test him out. He came under it like a ferret and grabbed me round the waist to take me to the floor. We landed on our sides, but I was stronger and got on top of him. I tried to smash his head off the floor but his neck muscles were too strong and he seethed, 'You dirty bastard.' I pulled my hands free and clubbed him with two heavy shots. My hands were bleeding, as my knuckles had little stones embedded in them from the gravel in the car park. I was firmly in charge. He said he'd had enough, but I wasn't satisfied – I wanted to prove that I could finish him at his fittest, so I continued to wade into him twice more with my pounding, bloody fists. When it got really serious, I got up and started walking away. Then I heard him shout out to me, 'Richy, Richy.' I went back to look at him, laid there covered in blood. He couldn't get up. He said,

'Richy, you can't leave me here, not like this!' So I picked him up, hoisted him over my shoulder and took him to his car. I'm a fair man and I don't take liberties – once a man is done, he's done and that's it. Although the fight ended in some sort of truce, I have never been able to have a lot of respect for Davo due to the way he couldn't keep his trap shut about other matters. But let's leave it at that.

The Davo aggro may have been put to bed, but it wasn't long before I bumped into another old adversary, Big Bri. We were out celebrating Vul's birthday one night when I spotted him in a pub. Buggery hell, he was with his woman and another couple. I kept it to myself and pretended I had never seen him. They finished their drinks and left. That was that, I thought. But as soon as I walked out on the street a few minutes later, BANG! The crafty bastard! Big Bri had caught me with a massive right hand. There was a blinding flash of light before my eyes, followed by a drum roll in my head. He hits me again, forcing me back against the window, before following up with another smartly aimed blow to my chin. If there was nothing behind me, I think I'd have gone down. While this was happening, my mates were stood in mortified shock. Then my mate Wally jumped in and pushed him back. Bri shouted, 'Come on then, I'll fight the fucking lot of ya!' Then my other mate, Ryao, shouted, 'Right then, let them.'

There were a few pubs close together with glass fronts

and everyone was at the windows eyeballing what was going on. We should have charged £5 a head! As I walked towards Big Bri, my legs were still like jelly and my mouth was cut and bleeding. We were in the main street that runs through the centre of town and all the cars had stopped because they couldn't get past the gathering crowd. At first, we both missed with a few sharp bursts of wild punches. Then, BANG! I catch him with a full left hook and he goes down like a ferret down a hole after a rabbit. When that punch landed, I broke my hand. It simultaneously broke his jaw. As Big Bri went reeling backwards towards the ground, I saw his eyes rolling around; it looked pretty funny to be honest. His head bounced off the tarmac road. I dragged him off the road and got on top of him and let him have it. When I got off him, I spat the blood that was swamping my mouth into his face.

I then looked down at him. He really looked like he was dying ... shit! The ambulance arrived in about a minute and they put an oxygen mask straight on him. I could see the life draining out of him. You see, this is the problem with street fighting – we are only flesh and blood at the end of the day. At hospital, he was very close to dying. I was, in truth, worried. Luckily, the big bastard pulled through. Would you believe that he wanted to press charges afterwards? But I had too many witnesses to say he'd started it and the CPS kicked it out. Years later, I bumped into him at a party. Everyone thought it would kick off again. We both looked at each other, but then we smiled and shook hands. It's all water under the bridge now and we have a mutual respect for each other.

Such incidents furthered my reputation on the streets. I came out of a nightclub in Middlesbrough one night and a lad came up to me and said, 'I've seen you fight three times and you are fucking awesome, I'd just like to shake your hand.' I shook his hand and he looked over the moon, then he went back to his girlfriend and they walked off. That's always a nice exchange, but unfortunately there are plenty of twats in this world all too ready to take the piss. I was working a bar with Vul one night when a bunch of Middlesbrough lads came in. We tried to be friendly with them but they weren't having any of it. The manager was beside himself with worry. We made some phone calls and got a posse of lads down. We turned the music off and I went over with the lads behind me. I said, 'Right, clever cunts, it's your choice. KICK OFF OR FUCK OFF.' I repeated myself even louder: 'KICK OFF OR FUCK OFF.' Now that the odds were even, they didn't fancy their chances, so we started taking their drinks away and they all got up and left. The way I see it, why act like a cunt if you aren't prepared to fight like a man?

One night on the door, we got a call from upstairs when some trouble had broken out. I was the first one on the scene. One of our doormen, Frankie, was on top of a lad on the dance floor, whilst about five of the lad's mates were kicking the fuck out of him. I dropped the first one I came on like a sack of potatoes. Then I waded into his pals, giving them all a fucking hammering. Frankie afterwards said that they were booting him for about a minute, but the fucking DJ never put the call out, so we couldn't get up there until someone ran down and told us. I had some nasty words for the DJ at the end of the night and he filled up with tears and packed in working there. He certainly learned a lesson that night.

Pubs and clubs were one thing, as you could always control the area, but raves were a different matter. I worked on the door at a rave venue in Stockton for four weeks. There were a lot of dodgy characters in there and I could feel something was going to happen so packed it in. I went back a week later, just as a customer. As we were stood in the queue, two bouncers popped their heads out the door and pointed at me before closing the door. I was only in there for one hour and thought I was in danger so I left with a friend. As we went out, a car full of strange-looking geezers pulled up. I never looked at them, but I knew they were staring at me and I thought I was going to take a bullet. We jumped in the motor and left. The car with the blokes in followed us for a few miles and then turned round and headed back. That was my finish with those paranoid places.

Not long after, Vul's cousin Eddie died in a car crash. I was gutted. We attended the funeral, which was

A card sent to me by Charles Bronson, Britain's most notorious prisoner. I've challenged him to a bout when he's released.

SOME MEN ARE JUST BORN TO FIGHT.
IT'S IN THERE BLOOD. THEY CAN'T DO NOTHING ABOUT IT. THEY HAVE TO FIGHT.
A FIGHTER ISN'T NECESSARY A PSYCHO OR A THUG - FAR FROM IT! MOST FIGHTERS ARE GENTLEMEN - MEN OF PRIDE. MEN OF HONOUR.
PUT A BABY IN THERE ARMS AND THEY CRY WITH JOY LIKE ANY MAN.
BUT IF YOU FUCK WITH A FIGHTER, YOU'VE GOT TO EXPECT THE CONSEQUENCES. YOUR GUNNA GET HURT. YOU MAY EVEN DIE.
NO MAN IS INVINCIBLE, EVEN THE FIGHTERS AT TIMES FEEL DEFEAT, SOME EVEN DIE.
BUT BET YOUR ARSE ON IT.
IF THEY DON'T DIE -- THERE COMING BACK FOR MORE!
RICHY HORSLEY IS ONE OF THESE SPECIAL BREED OF MEN. AND I'M HONOURED TO KNOW THE MAN
"MAX RESPECT"

PS/- BUT HE STILL COULDN'T BEAT MY ROCKY THE egg! :)

BRONSON 1314 LIFE H.M.P. DURHAM (SPECIAL CAGE) 2-001

In the ring with Tony Louis …

Above: Fighting and trying to land an uppercut in close.

Below: It's all over after 90 seconds, as Louis is counted out.

Close friends from the world of boxing. *Above*, with Kevin Bennett, Commonwealth Lightweight champion and, *below*, with Michael Hunter, British Super Bantamweight champion.

Some of my best friends.

Above left: My lifelong friends Tommy Barff and his lovely sister Donna.

Above right: With Collo, who took care of a bully for me when I was a kid.

Below: Boys' night out, with Watto and Kenny.

Above: With Wally, left, and bestelling author, Cass Pennant.

Below left: With the late Tony Lambrianou who, in his lifetime, was a member of the notorious Kray firm.

Below right: With Harry Marsden.

Above: Donna and Terry as youngsters.

Below: At a centre for birds of prey. I love all birds (the feathered variety!) but particularly love the power and majesty of these creatures.

Above: With Mark, who lost his brave battle with leukaemia. Me and Brian Cockerill carried the coffin at his funeral.

Below: In Scotland, I bumped into the actor Paul Kaye while he was taking a break from filming his TV series *2000 Acres of Skye*.

THE AMATEUR BOXING ASSOCIATION OF ENGLAND LTD

Patron: H.R.H. THE DUKE OF EDINBURGH, K.G., K.T.

President: LORD OAKSEY

RICHARD HORSLEY

of the

HARTLEPOOL BOYS WELFARE

*Has passed the Amateur Boxing Association Coaching Examination
and has qualified as an Assistant Coach.*

RbHarvey .... HON. SECRETARY

DATE 8TH NOV. 1998 TYNE TEES WEAR .... ASSOCIATION

Above: I now train boys how to box.

Below: Pounding the heavy bag – I've still got to keep myself in shape.

packed. Later, I was in a boozer with Vul when Big John, who was 6ft 4in and weighed 18 stone, walked in along with his pals. Vul told me about Big John taking the piss in Eddie's pub after he died; he wouldn't pay for drinks and wanted a lock-in, he was properly trying it on. As they finished their drinks, I went and stood in front of the door. As Big John got near me, I struck him with a right hand that nearly took his head off. You'd think he had been shot in the head by a sniper. He was laid flat out and, as usual, an ambulance was called. As they carried him out, one of his mates came back in and said to me, 'Do it to me, go on, fucking try it with me.' I obliged and flattened him as well. At least Big John had someone to go to the hospital with in the ambulance.

I went back to work with Mick Sorby, who I always got on well with and respected. Whenever people came in a pub and we were on the door, they'd think twice about starting anything. I started to do a few light weights just to tone my body up. I was now weighing in at a respectable 18 stone. Mick and I did loads of jobs together. We'd go to drug dealers' houses and slap them around or punch them up a bit, whatever was needed, and take the drug money off them. They were only scumbags anyway, so it made no difference to us or anyone else for that matter. We once met a dealer in a car park because we pretended we wanted to do business with him. He was driving around in a nice flash BMW and he was supposed to be a bobby's toot – a spy for the police. We took his car off him and told him to fuck off before he got hurt. The BMW was a ringer so the fella couldn't go to the police. We drove around in it for a day and then thought we'd better get rid of it and sold it on for two grand. A nice little earner, as was beating people up for money. So and so wants to know if you'll break so and so's jaw for £500. Jobs like that were always coming my way. There were limits though. I would never go to anyone's house when there were children present. No way!

As our reputations grew, we started to attract all sorts of characters. One geezer turned up in the town out of the blue, wanting to meet Mick and me. We met him in a pub and he started pulling bundles of money out, trying to impress us saying he was this and that. He was full of shit. The dickhead even said he was an expert knife thrower, very impressive. We took his money off him and told him to fuck off and to never try to get in touch with us again. We counted the bundles and it came to six grand. Lovely!

Another oddball was a lad called Stevie who worked the door for Mick. He was a proper Billy Liar – we used to call him 'Stevie Tallstory' or 'Bang, Bang'. Almost every time you seen him, he'd say, 'I done these two blokes earlier. You should have been there, I just went bang, bang and they were both out.' These fights were just his imagination. He liked a drink and when he drank he had a wagging tongue and loose lips and liked to be loud. His ex-wife was living with an old work mate of mine. I bumped into him one day and he told me that Stevie was badmouthing me. I went to Stevie's flat but he wouldn't open the door. He was pretending he wasn't in but I knew he was because I could hear him through the letterbox. I shouted that I was going to remove his head from his body for badmouthing me and I'd have him within a couple of days. I didn't know it, but he'd just been cashed up for a compensation claim. Soon enough I got a call from a middleman telling me that Stevie was very sorry. I was invited around the middleman's house, where he handed me a nice wad of money and said, 'Here's two grand for your trouble.' I said, 'Tell him he's OK, but to keep his big fat mouth shut in future.' Another nice little earner, I'm sure you will agree.

Amid all the money making, I started going out with a mixed-race girl. Every week, I'd see her on the dance floor in the nightclub bopping away. I'd stare over and she'd smile at me. She was gorgeous with hair as black as a raven's wing. I asked to take her home and we hit it off straight away. We fell in love. Her name was Linda and she had two kids, Ashleigh and Grant. I was as happy as a pig in shit. I asked her to marry me, and she accepted. But we wanted to do things very quietly, so only had eight people present at the wedding, and Mick Sorby, the Best Man. We went for a drink after and I phoned people up and told them I'd been married.

They were all shocked and I think they thought I was pulling their legs. They all said the same thing: 'Why wasn't I invited?'

Meanwhile, the fighting was as rife as ever. When you get a big reputation, it becomes hard to know what is going on: people start spreading lies, and you get associated with things that you had nothing to do with. Bri Cockerill was supposed to be telling people he wanted to fight me. I was getting a bit pissed off with the rumours. Everyone seemed to be talking about it. I phoned my pal from Boro called Ste Shannon and asked him what the word on the street was, and he confirmed the rumours.

'OK then, tell him I'll fight him. I'm scared of no fucker.' This never came to anything and when I met Bri not long after, we became good mates and have been ever since. To make things even more complicated, the Big Irish guy who was imprisoned for those stabbings was let out. He acted as a go-between and organised a meeting in a pub. We sat down and got it all sorted out. Maori told me later that he had a Magnum tucked in his waistband, just in case. We then went to a few bars with Irish while he was on his home leave as a goodwill gesture. Now unbeknown to Big Irish, his wife had been seeing this big ginger lad on the sly, who so happened to be standing near us with his pal. I noticed they were getting clever with Irish. I saw Maori's face and enquired, 'What's up?'

He said, 'Irish is gonna stab these two. He's got a blade under his coat.'

I said, 'Mind this drink,' and walked over. I went over to one, and BANG! He went down. Then I turned to the big ginger one. BANG! He went down straight away. He was in a bad way and was rushed into hospital. I didn't realise how serious he was; he nearly died and had a blood transfusion. It's ironic that I only intervened so that Irish wouldn't carve them up, but in the end I nearly ended up killing the lad with my bare hands.

The confusion got worse on a particular night during a lock-in with Mick. There was banging on the door. It was the armed police draped in their bulletproof vests, wanting our names. We found out why a few days later. There had been a lad over the road waiting in the shadows with a gun, waiting for me to come out so he could kill me. Someone must have known what he was going to do and phoned the police. The cops went down and, sure enough, he was there with a shooter so they nabbed him. When he was in jail, he got his nose bitten off. So there is some justice in the world.

Not long after this, I drove down to an estate with Maori and another lad to meet some guys who we had some ongoing trouble with. We got out of the Land Rover and walked over to them. Before we could say anything, they pulled out guns and started firing at us. I could hear bullets whooshing past my head as we charged back to the Land Rover. We jumped in and sped away like Michael Schumacher. All the windows got shot out. We got away OK, but the lad with us took a shot to the shoulder. He was sat in the back, white as a ghost, and looked like he was going into shock. We sped off to the hospital and dropped him off in emergency. We must have looked a right sight pulling up with all the windows shot in. Maori and I were lucky to get away unscathed, but we did walk around with Don King-style hair for a few weeks after that.

I went with a few lads to see a bloke who owed a lot of money to someone. Sorry, I can't go into details, but you know how it is. We found him alone. The lads gave him an unmerciful beating, thrashing him with big fuck-off sticks. I went out of the room, as I didn't want to watch. The guy sounded like he was in terrible pain, so I thought I'd better put him out of his misery. As I went back in the room, he was unrecognisable; his arm was snapped in half and the bone was sticking out through the skin. My stomach turned over. I went over and hit him on the side of the jaw with a big right and he went out like a light – at least he was out of pain. I didn't go on another one of those jobs again. Out of the few lads who were there, one is doing life for murder and another one is dead. It's a short-term game to be in.

I was starting to think that if I stayed on the door, sooner or later I was going to end up in prison or dead, so I was thinking about chucking it. But then again, I was still finding trouble in pubs where I wasn't working.

One time I went out to celebrate my birthday with a group of lads. Everyone was buying me double whisky chasers. I was reluctant, at first, to drink the whisky because I knew I'd be drunk in no time. But once it went down, I got the taste for it and washed every pint down with a straight double whisky. We were all getting into the swing of it, and by 9.30 I was mortal drunk. Now that's as far as my memory of that night goes, so the rest of this story is reliant upon other sources. One of the lads with us was also called Richy; he had caused trouble with some lads who were on the dance floor enjoying themselves. He decided to get stuck into them. These lads were everywhere we went after this, and again and again Richy was always straight over fighting with them. Now I don't know about you, but if I was out on somebody's birthday, the last thing that I'd want to do is fight because it spoils the night. If I was sober, I guarantee there'd have been no trouble because I would have nipped it straight in the bud. After all, these lads were from out of town and were having a good time before he started chew with them. As the end of the night approached, I was propped up against the bar because I was just about legless. Everyone had gone home drunk or gone elsewhere because it was too quiet where we were, but I said I was staying put. There was only me and Darren left. In the meantime, all these lads that Richy had started trouble with came back to the club I was in to get revenge. At 1.45am, a crowd of thirty geezers were outside the nightclub asking for 'Richy'. The doormen wouldn't let them in because they knew there was going to be trouble and they didn't want the place smashed up. A bouncer came over and said, 'Richy, there's about thirty blokes outside want you and they're looking for trouble.' Well, of course, I was *not* the 'Richy' they were looking for. But I told the bouncer I was coming out and he went back downstairs.

I took no notice of the bouncer's warning that I would get killed, and started down the stairs to the entrance and the angry mob. As I got out into the street, I was attacked with bottles over the head, punches, kicks and elbows. I was fighting on memory, as I fought tooth and nail and, as my punches were landing, they started hitting the deck like dominoes. The bouncers were stood watching the action open-mouthed from the bay window. I was taking a beating and getting attacked from behind with bottles being smashed over the back of my head. This time it was my turn to go down like a lead balloon; I got kicked unconscious. Later, I was told that my head was jumped on and kicked about like a football. I was told I put seven of them in the hospital, but the lad watching from the bay window said he counted nine, so I gave a good account of myself considering the situation.

After being examined, I was put into a ward in the hospital. I remember waking up and staring at the ceiling, thinking something wasn't right. As my eyes started to focus and my mind started to wake up, I realised where I was. What the fuck was I doing here? As I sat up, the pillow came with me because it was stuck to the back of my head with congealed blood. I shouted for the nurse. I asked her what I was doing in there. She said I was admitted with head injuries and that if I hadn't been so drunk, I would have died. She asked if I wanted any breakfast and I said, 'Yes.' As she went to get me some, I quickly put my clothes on and left. I looked like the Elephant Man.

That was some fucking birthday present. The street had CCTV cameras on it so I knew the coppers would be studying it. I also knew that the nightclub had a camera on the door, so I made a phone call to get my hands on the tape. But the police beat me to it. People came to see me after to ask if I wanted to put bullets in these people, but I said, 'No.' I said I would fight any of them or all of them one at a time, but nothing came of it. Time is a great healer and I don't bear grudges against any of them. Shit happens. If you live by the sword, you die by the sword and that's the way it is. You've got to accept it. The police eventually turned up and asked about the fight, but I said I couldn't remember anything. They asked if I wanted to press charges if they found them, but I said, 'No chance,' and told them to forget it. I would rather have died outside that club than grass anyone up. I bet the filth enjoyed themselves watching that tape over tea and biscuits. I bet they wore the fucker out.

CHAPTER 17

FIRE ARM

A nice respite from all the fighting came when I trained for a driving test when I was 28. One day I just fancied learning, so I booked some lessons with a family friend called Tony, who ran his own driving school. The driving school had a good pass rate; I had about a dozen lessons with him, less than full price, which was cushty. When the day of my test arrived, I was nervous and had an hour's lesson to calm my nerves before the real thing. I coped with it very well and stayed relaxed throughout. After we arrived back, the examiner said the magical words, 'I'm pleased to tell you, you've passed.'

Trouble soon popped up again though when I went to a nightclub in Redcar with a couple of lesbians I knew through my mate Andy. One of them was so butch that she looked just like a man. While she was dancing, I could see a lad starting to get clever with her. Something was bound to happen. I waited until it was going to kick off and went over. The lad squared up to me in a boxer's stance. I tore straight into him and hit him with about four short, fast punches. He lay there unable to move, covered in claret. The bouncers were pals of Bri Cockerill, so they left me alone and chucked out the prick I had done. That was the end of that story, but a bit later on at New Year I got caught up in trouble because of the dykes yet again. I had taken some ecstasy drugs off a dealer in a pub, given him a good slap in the process, and decided to give them to the lesbians, as they were into that scene. Little did I know that they were also getting their gear off a father-and-son team who dealt to the dealer that I had slapped. Word got back to them and they ended up setting the lesbians up for a police raid, as they thought they had fucked them over. Unluckily for me, I wandered into their house to say hello just as they were getting raided. To top it off, I had a stun gun in my pocket, which I had confiscated off a guy in one of the pubs I was working the night before. The pigs stripsearched me, found the gun, and arrested me and took me to the station. It went to court, where on my solicitor's advice I pleaded guilty. I got a fine, but the two lesbians ended up taking all the blame for the drugs, and each got 18 months inside.

I still blame my fine on the stupid father who set the lesbians up. Quite conveniently, I bumped into him one morning outside some busy shops. I cuffed him with a right to the body and a left into his smarmy face. He never went down but staggered and ran over the road. He started mouthing off threats about what he was going to have done to me. I was told later that, as a consequence of our short and sweet reunion, he had a smashed rib and broken nose. The punk also put a figure on my head. My mate Maori made a few phone calls and found out there was an underworld hitman coming from Newcastle to put one in me, but he managed to get it stopped.

As soon as that little episode came to a close, I was rocketed into another situation one night when I bumped into an old acquaintance on a pub crawl. Ron K, as he was known, was a short and powerful man, who had just been released from prison. We were getting on OK to begin with but, as he got drunk, he started getting on people's nerves shouting about how hard he was. Then he shouted to me, 'Oi, you, outside.' Now I thought the prick was just joking, but he wasn't. 'I'm the best fourteen stone you'll come across,' he screamed. So off comes my coat and we step outside.

The pub had a glass front so everyone could see us. I have to admit I loved the feeling of having a crowd. Without any hesitation, he came straight at me. BANG! I catch him with a short, powerful left hook. He folded like a ten-pound note and hit the ground with the finesse of a smashed egg. What an anti-climax. You have to think of the crowd in these situations, so I bent over him and put about four face-bursting rights on his chin. He was whisked away to another planet. When the ambulance stretchered him away about 15 minutes later with an oxygen mask on, he was still sleeping soundly. His jaw was shattered in four places, so they had to put a fancy steel plate in with screws to fix it. I had no sympathy for him because he brought it all on himself with his big loud mouth.

Yet I was also realising that this intensity of fighting couldn't go on. I went for a private sitting with a clairvoyant, who sensed that I was a fighter. He got hold of my hands and said, 'I can't tell you to stop fighting, but if you continue and you don't start pulling your punches, I can see you killing someone, someday.' I had already had a few lucky escapes with people hovering at death's door and took that as a serious warning. I slowed down and took a back seat. Linda had filed for a divorce on the grounds of 'unreasonable behaviour'. I had to have a sit down and have a think about what I was doing with my life.

The situation of one of my mates, H, really brought things home to me. He had got into some trouble in Lincoln, but his father wouldn't stand as a guarantor for him over the deal. He'd been treated badly by his father all his life and had a stammer because of it. So when he wouldn't stand guarantor he was pushed over the edge and went round his father's house. A big argument erupted and H pulled out a gun and shot him three times at point blank range: in the head, chest and kneecap. His father was lying in a pool of blood. H must have known he was going to get life, and thought, Fuck it, I've had enough. He put the gun to his temple and pulled the trigger. The father miraculously survived, but H died. It was a sad time for all concerned. The last time I had seen him alive, he had made us both bacon and toast and we'd had a chinwag. I think of it like the last supper and still have some fond memories of him.

It was all too much, so I packed the door work in to get away from all the trouble. But the faster I tried to get away from it, the faster trouble came after me. One time I was out in a pub with my mates Mick, Freddie, Peter and Johnny. I went to the toilet while they went to the bar, where there was a skinhead looking the worse for drink. He mumbled, 'What's your name?' I told him and his chest plumed out another foot. He put his hand out for me to shake it. Peter had followed me in and was watching the proceedings. I went to shake the affable skinhead's hand, but he pulled it away and slurred, 'Dry your fucking hand, first.' What a cheeky cunt! I planted a left hook on his chin and as he went down he cracked his head off one of the urinals. He was laid out with blood spewing from his head. 'Dry your fucking head, first,' I laughed at the floored skinhead. The slurring skinhead recovered but that was the moment when I thought I had better stop going out drinking as well or, like the clairvoyant said, 'someone would die'.

I started to turn my life around for the better and tried to instil a bit of stability and balance back. I wanted to leave that part of my life behind. The leopard wanted to ditch its spots! The divorce finally went through, although a few months later Linda and I ended up going out again, but only as boyfriend–girlfriend. It was a case of can't live with her, can't live without her. We were together for eight years. In the meantime I was beginning to realise how lucky I was when I started sponsoring a girl in Ecuador, South America, after seeing an advert on TV about the Third World. Every time the advert came on, I saw the pain and suffering in the children's eyes. Jomayra's life is much better these days and she is getting an education. If she becomes ill, a doctor will see her due to the sponsorship. I have been her sponsor since 1997 and it's a very rewarding experience. We exchange letters and Jomayra always tells me how grateful she is and calls me her foster parent. I send her two presents a year, as well as cards and photos. She is now fourteen years old, and the difference in her over the seven years from the first photo to the present one is amazing. It's great being a part of another family's life that live on the other side of the world. It opens your eyes as to how people in other countries live.

I enjoyed being compassionate, which made a nice break from the fighting. One day I was looking through the paper and saw a picture of a woman who had had her pet African Grey parrot stolen. Funnily enough, I then got a phone call from Brian Cockerill asking for my help in respect of this stolen parrot as he was good friends with the lady in the paper. My mate Ste had a pet shop and said he had just been offered such a parrot. The lad offering the parrot for sale was a friend of Mick's, and so Mick and I went to see him. We soon discovered that he had sold the parrot on to a dealer for £200. Armed with the dealer's address, we paid him little visit. On finding him, we told him the parrot was stolen and that we wanted it back for its owner. We asked him very kindly to go and get the bird and to bring it to my house ... or to face the consequences! He looked as sick as a parrot. He came around the next day with the parrot, and we went around the real owner's house. Her and the kids were over the moon. The bloke told her the story of how he came across it and she couldn't thank me enough. I received a follow-up phone call from Brian Cockerill, who thanked me and said he owed me a favour. A few days later, the newspaper ran the story, along with a photo, of the woman being reunited with her parrot, but I told her to keep my name out of it, which she did. I do love happy endings.

If I was going to get a truly peaceful life, I had to get out of Hartlepool, so I got another job installing heavy electric cables around the country. The first job I took was at ICI, Wilton, which I was on for a few months. I really wanted to make a go of it, and stuck at it, even though it was hard graft. The safety code was stringent, and at all times you had to wear a hard hat, safety boots, goggles, overalls and gloves. Even on hot days when your goggles were steaming up with sweat and you couldn't see, you weren't supposed to take them off. The cables I worked with aren't the little piddling things for domestic use. The ones I'm on about are always on big round drums; once you got the drum in the exact place you wanted it, you put a jack either side with a steel bar running through the drum and then it would be jacked off the floor ready to pull the cable off. Sometimes, the cable would go in a trench or up a riser, but mainly it was tied on to giant racks and it all had to be held in place with cleats. It was proper hard work, as the big drums can weigh as much as nine tons. There were plenty of hazards in this line of work. Once, when I was working in Edinburgh, we were rolling a drum that weighed about six tons when it ran over my foot! My steel toe collapsed and came through the side of my boot. My toes came up like puddings. I was lucky because if it was another inch over I would have lost my toes. On another job, we were working under a canal and the tunnels went on for a couple of miles. After we renewed the cable we had to make a hasty retreat as there were always toxic gasses being released.

My job has taken me the length and breadth of the UK: Barnsley, Manchester, Widness, Newcastle, Reading,

London, Derby, Middlesex, Scotland, Portsmouth, Southampton, Bournemouth, Rhyl, Cardiff and plenty of other places. I even once had a piss on the roof of the Hilton Hotel, in Park Lane, London, when we were putting some cable in. I was bursting and the toilet was too far away. Sometimes, there'd only be half a dozen cables to pull in and once you'd done that, you were off somewhere else. One day you could be in Leeds and the next in London; I liked it better like that instead of being stuck in the same place. Once we went to a job at Derby for about six weeks. I had a look for the house me and the family stayed at back in 1975–1976. It was in Boyer Street but it had been pulled down and new houses had been built. Nothing stays the same. While I was at Derby, I got a phone call off Maori. It was bad news. His son Mark had just died of leukaemia, only four weeks past his 18th birthday. It was another heartbreak. Mark was a lovely lad. We – Wally, Dickie and me – all went home for the funeral. It was a very sad time.

One of the main benefits of moving around was that I could go drinking again without getting into trouble. One time we were staying above a pub in St Helens. We went downstairs for a drink, and I spotted a face I recognised. But it wasn't an old opponent from Hartlepool. It was the well-known rugby player, Andy Gregory. I went over and said, 'Hello, Andy. You don't know me, but I'm working round here and would just like to say hello.' He shook my hand and asked where I was from. Then in another pub I heard, 'Not you again.' It was Andy. Later, in a nightclub, I spotted him at the bar so I went over and tapped him on the shoulder, When he turned round I said, 'Are you fucking following me?' He started laughing and repeated, 'Not you again.' He had a good sense of humour, and was a really nice bloke.

Even when there was a bit of trouble, I kept things as quiet as possible. On the job in Liverpool, there was a new mush that had started for us called Trevor. He thought he knew everything, so I called him 'Know It All Trevor'. On the way down there on a Monday morning, he did everybody's head in. As soon as we got on the job, he started running around like he was the boss and talking to people as if they were idiots. He was a cheeky cunt. I let him get away with a couple of remarks, but when he said another thing I thought I'd teach him a lesson. I later spotted Mr Know It All up in what is called a cherry picker. A cherry picker is simply a mobile gantry tower that is like being on the end of a giant moveable arm; you've probably seen them around when the local council use them for replacing streetlight bulbs and the like. Mr Know It All was up there with a lad called Varley. I shouted to Varley, 'Bring that fucking cherry picker down here, now!' I stood and watched as my prey was being moved in my direction. As he was getting closer and closer, his face became whiter and whiter. As soon as he reached me, I dragged him out of his harness and nearly took his head off with a persuasive slap. It was so powerful that it spun him around so fast that, for a few seconds, he looked like Michael Jackson doing one of his routines. For a couple of days after that, he walked around with what looked like a big purple birthmark down half his face. He never talked to me out of turn again.

Another benefit of travelling was getting to know the history of various places. When we went to London I took a day off and spent a full day in the Tower of London. I love history, and the day passed really quickly. After that, we went to Scotland for six weeks to put the cable in on a place in the middle of the Firth of Forth. One of the local lads called Gregor started telling me a bit of Scottish history about William Wallace and the like. I enjoyed our chats. A couple of years later, he emigrated to Australia, from where he still sends a Christmas card every year, even if it does arrive in January. We stayed in Dunfermline, right opposite the abbey where Robert the Bruce is buried. There is a story that Robert the Bruce was born in Hartlepool, so I went to his grave to pay my respects to a fellow hard bastard from the North East.

The other lads started getting into the history too, so one day Dickie, Wally, and I went for a historic day out to Bannockburn where the Scots won their fight for independence in 1314. We went in the Visitors Centre where Robert the Bruce's helmet and chainmail were on display, bolted to the wall on the end of a small chain. I was really excited when the curator allowed me the privilege of wearing this warrior's helmet and chainmail. I'll tell you what, it was bloody heavy. I wouldn't have wanted to go 12 rounds with that kit on. I had my photo taken and we took a camcorder with us, so we have the whole day on film. From there we went to visit the William Wallace Monument, which I would very much recommend. They have Wallace's sword in a glass case. It's the actual sword that was taken off him in 1305 when he was captured by the sheriff of Dumbarton. The sight of such implements of war conjures up many things in the imagination. I had nothing but respect for these ageless warriors.

The bloke who owned the cable firm was a millionaire and once you got to know him he was a nice fella. He owned houses, clubs and businesses. In one of his clubs the manager and manageress were taking him to the cleaners, saying that stuff was being stolen, but they were behind it all along. They were a pair of cheeky, loud-mouthed bastards who always had to have the last word. He wanted them out but wanted to do it legally, so he got papers drawn up for the manager to sign. He knew he wouldn't sign them and that there'd be trouble, so he phoned me and asked for my help. After we agreed on a price for the job, he came and picked me up and we went along. When I got to the club in question, I told the manager to sit down and ordered, 'Listen to me and listen good, if you open your mouth just once to speak or answer back when I'm speaking, I'm gonna break your fucking jaw! Now listen to what that man has to say and sign the papers. Do you understand?' He knew the game was up and mumbled, 'Yes.' His woman must of known the game was up as well because she never came into the room, preferring to stay out of the way. The papers were duly signed with no problems and they were evicted.

All the history visits must have made me sentimental, as not long after I wanted to get myself my own piece of history. I had noticed a beautiful pot statue behind the bar of a bare-knuckle fighter and asked the millionaire club-owner about it. He raised an eyebrow and said that plenty of people wanted it. I said that I would like to buy it but, as an act of generosity, he gave me it as a present. It still stands tall and proud in my bedroom. The boxing promoter Frank Maloney has the exact same one in his house, as I saw it one day on the TV programme *Through The Keyhole*. He must have very good taste.

CHAPTER 18

IT'S NICE TO BE IMPORTANT, BUT IT'S IMPORTANT TO BE NICE

I ended up working on the cable installations for three years. I enjoyed that time and generally avoided trouble, although the little rascal had a habit of turning up from time to time. One night I was enjoying a few drinks on my own in a pub away from home. I got talking with the doorman about boxing, and everything was fine. But then a bunch of pissed people walk in. I was stood at the end of the bar minding my own business, just deciding whether to have one more for the road or to go. As I looked up I noticed I was being stared at. Five lads, all in their mid-twenties, were slowly getting closer and closer. Instinct told me they were going to have a pop at me. Knowing how important it is to be the first to the fight, I started up right off, and belted the biggest one with a cranking right hand. BOSH! He was out for a nice sleep. Always deck the strongest of the group to send out a clear message to the other pricks. I blasted his mate, who was stood to the right of him, with a beautiful, classic left hook bang on the chin. It rocked him so much that he was out of it before he hit the deck. Why bother stopping now, I thought to myself, so for good measure I put the third one away into cloud cuckoo land. The doormen arrived just as I had just put the last one of the five to bed. All the time, I had been expecting to be punched from the side or bashed over the head with something, but luckily for me that never happened. The next day, my elbow was swollen right up and I could hardly move it. For the next week, I was being woken up during the night with jolts of pain in my elbow. I decided to get an X-ray and found out that it was fractured, but I decided against a pot – plaster cast – as it would have driven me fucking mad.

Nevertheless, this scrap reinvigorated my interest in the world of fighting, so one night I went with a few lads to watch a friend of mine fight at a boxing show in Sunderland. The guest of honour was Ernie Shavers, the American heavyweight puncher from the 1970s. I used to love watching him fight, as he was one of the hardest-hitting heavies of all time. I couldn't believe it when I saw him there. I shook the great man's giant of a hand and asked him who was the best fighter he ever fought and without hesitation he said, 'Muhammad Ali.' There was a professional photographer there and he took a photo of us with Ernie. About a week later, the photos arrived in the post. I had them enlarged and sent all the lads a copy each. I got mine framed and it hung it by the stairs, where it proudly sits to this day.

I got to know the coach, Graham, at the Boys Welfare. He invited me to go to the gym and watch a few sparring sessions. While I watched, it started getting in my bones again. I decided to help out with the youngsters. I went on a coaching course over in Sunderland in order to get qualified. I hadn't done any training for God knows how long and after the first day, I was wiped out. The next day, I had to go through it all again and was as stiff as a board. I was sweating bucket loads and one of the instructors said to me, 'You should leave the beer alone the night before you come here.' But I hadn't had any beer – I was just unfit! The second part of the course was held two weeks later. My partner throughout the course was Neil Fannan, whom I knew from the old days. When we were going through various blocks and combinations I'd slip a hard one into his ribs when he wasn't expecting it and he'd give me a 'you crafty cunt' look. Then just when I'd relax and forget about it, BANG! I'd cop the same treatment and I'd look at him and he'd have a big cheesy grin all over his face. A few weeks later, we got our results: both of us had passed with flying colours.

The 1998–99 season was a unique time in Hartlepool amateur boxing, especially for the Boys Welfare.

Everybody seemed to come together from far and wide and we had three boxers in the National ABA finals, a feat never done before in the town and never likely to be achieved again. We had some good lads, at senior and junior level. We had one lad from Tunisia called Mo who was raw and needed schooling, but he reached the National Novice Final where he was out pointed. There were two lads fresh out of the army who came for a change of scenery to box for our club, one of whom, Kevin Bennett, a light-welterweight, was an England International The other one was called Billy Bessey. Billy's brother, Chris, won six National ABA titles and regularly came up here to a boxing show or for a night out.

I enjoyed meeting all the younger lads, as they were all well mannered and a joy to be with. One night, I was sat in a club watching England v USA with two of the England boxers, Chris, who was the captain, and Ian Cooper. The Yank who Ian fought was called Jeff Lacy, who is currently the undefeated IBF Super Middleweight champion of the world. Ian gave me his vest and medal from the fight because he knew I appreciated anything like that. I framed the vest. Ian was a class act and reached the National ABA final at light middleweight in 1996, but went one better the next year and won the title at middleweight. I also became close friends with Kevin Bennett, as I liked the way he was polite and had nice manners. You go a long way when you have both, and he did. An old gypsy bare-knuckle fighter from years ago who lived round these parts used to say, 'It's nice to be important, but it's important to be nice.' After all, manners cost nothing.

We travelled all over the place for boxing shows. We especially had some good nights up in Scotland and we were always invited back. When we left clubs, there would be a crowd of people in the hall all clapping us off because they appreciated the quality of our boxers. They couldn't believe that one club would go up there and beat the best lads in Scotland. We always had a warm welcome and a couple came down to watch the lads in the ABAs. I took two junior boxers to the Royal Armouries at Leeds. We went up with another club from the town to share the petrol. Graham gave us a van to go in and said the brakes were a bit iffy but to just 'pump it and it'll stop'. I didn't like the sound of that.

On the way to pick the other club up, as I came to some traffic lights, I realised there were no brakes. I pumped and pumped and it still kept going. Incredibly, nothing came my way or it would have been a head-on collision. I was thinking, this cunt has set me up. Graham was always doing things like that. When I got to the club to pick Timmy and his boxers up I warned, 'Timmy, you can drive that, I'm not, it's a fucking death trap.' There were a few hair-raising moments that night and we were nearly killed a couple of times. When Timmy got out, his hair was grey!

199

I was still doing a bit on and off with the cable installations. I was working with a lad called Stewart Lithgo, who was Commonwealth Cruiserweight Champion in the 1980s; he brought the title back to Hartlepool from Australia when he knocked the champion out in the 11th round. He was as tough as old boots and was no mug. He fought Frank Bruno and big Frank hit him with his best shots and couldn't put Stewey down, it was stopped on cuts and Stewey protested furiously. He still runs and hits the bag a few times a week.

We had six boxers entered in the ABAs one year. Three of the lads fought the reigning national champions in the North East finals. At lightweight, Mo Helel lost a very close decision to Andy McLean. At light welterweight, Kevin Bennett beat Nigel Wright and at middleweight, Ian Cooper lost to John Pearce. With the others we had left, we realised we had a great chance of going all the way. The semi-finals were being held at the York Hall, in Bethnal Green, which promised to be a cracking show.

While we were there we went to Charlie Magri's sports shop and I had a good chat with him. Charlie was World Flyweight Champ in 1983 and his fights were all-action affairs. We talked about various fights and fighters and we got talking about George Feeney. Charlie said that he came to Hartlepool as an amateur and boxed George and won on points. When he and his coaches left the club, they were followed and chased by a gang of skinheads. He said they ran like hell with the skinheads in hot pursuit but they never got caught. Not surprisingly, Charlie never fought in Hartlepool again after that. When I got back home, I relayed that story back to George and he laughed his head off and said it was true. Most of the skins were his mates who never took too kindly to their pal getting beat.

I bought a blue pair of Everlast mini boxing gloves off him and they still hang in my car. After we left Charlie's shop, my pal Wally and I went to a pub called the Blind Beggar and had our dinner there. The pub, as most people know, was made famous as the place where East End gangster Ronnie Kray killed George Cornell with a bullet in the head. Strangely enough, the record playing on the jukebox at the time of the murder was by the Walker Brothers called 'The Sun Ain't Gonna Shine Any More' and as Ronnie was walking out he supposedly said, 'The sun ain't gonna shine any more for George.' The pub has changed a lot since then; it has been refurbished and is now a family pub. They do some nice scran.

We went back to the York Hall for the weigh-in and everyone started to think about the job in hand. As fight time approached, the place was packed out and everyone was buzzing. First up for us was Michael Hunter at bantamweight who boxed excellently and won by a wide decision. Then our light welterweight,

Kevin Bennett, was in action. I've never seen Benny more fired up than he was before this fight; he really did have the eye of the tiger. He tore straight into Jon Honney and ripped him apart. It was all over in 45 seconds. Our last man was at super heavyweight, Billy Bessey. He fought a big fella from Swindon and stopped him in the second round for a clean sweep. We had three in the National finals.

The biggest day ever in Hartlepool's amateur boxing history had arrived and a few coaches made the journey to the Barnsley Metrodome to support the lads. Ironically, our three boxers were up against three lads all from the same club, Repton, in London. They are the biggest amateur club in the country and have been for years. First up for us was a cracker, as Michael Hunter slugged it out with Andrew Wallace. Hunter came on strong in the last, making it anyone's title. The decision was announced as 10-9 to Hunter. Then we had Kevin Bennett against Danny Happe. I remember all the hair standing up on my neck with the noise and electricity as we were walking to the ring. Bennett was all over Happe in the first two rounds with Happe hardly throwing a punch because of the onslaught. He did connect a few times in the last round but we had Benny winning by a couple of points at the very least. But then the decision was announced as 9-8 to Happe. Benny said, 'I'm absolutely gutted. I won that fight, I'm sure of it. I've worked really hard all season and had no easy fights. I think I deserved a bit of luck and I didn't get it.' I knew the feeling. We were all gutted for Benny; if anyone deserved a title, it was him. Billy's brother Chris was in next at light middleweight. Chris beat K Hassaine from Balham, in London, by a score of 17-6. It was his sixth ABA title. He had won one at welterweight and five at light middleweight, putting him second on the all-time list with only John Lyon from St Helens ahead of him with eight titles.

The last fight of the night saw another Hartlepool v London encounter. It was the big men, the super heavyweights: Billy Bessey against Joe Young. It turned out to be a thriller and the crowd went wild. As the bell ended the second round, Young hit Bessey twice. Billy wobbled on unsteady legs back to the corner. Young should have been disqualified, which I think he would have been if Billy had stayed on his stool, but Graham said, 'Go out and win it the proper way.' Billy's nose was bust and there was blood all over his face. When they went back at it, Young was looking for the winner when Billy pulled out a big one, which landed flush on the chin. BANG! Young was counted out in the third to spark delirious scenes.

Billy said it was the best punch he'd ever thrown, and the best moment of his life. He and his brother Chris wrote themselves into the record books, not only as ABA Champs, but also as one of only a handful of brothers to win titles on the same night. In the local paper Graham said, 'I'm so pleased for him, he has lived in his brother's shadow throughout his career and to win an ABA title is a tremendous and fitting reward for him.' Underneath that feature, it read, 'It was also a fitting reward for the Welfare coaching team of Reed, Neil Fannan and Richy Horsley, who guided three boxers through to the grand finals and ended the illustrious competition with two magnificent champions.'

Perhaps my biggest influence over the lads centred on a humble vest. I gave Billy one of my old Nike ones to replace his old white vest and, as I gave it to him, I joked that if he inherits a bit of my power from it he'll be undefeated. All joking aside, when he wore it, he notched 13 wins in a row including the ABA title. So a bit of the Horsley magic did rub off on him.

CHAPTER 19

SUICIDE IS PAINFUL

My love affair with Scotland continued when I took
Linda up there for a holiday. After finishing a cable job
in Cardiff at the Millennium Stadium, the work had
dried up and a few of us had got laid off for a while. In
my first week off I took a trip down the bookies, and
picked some horses out in an each-way accumulator
bet. That night in the digs, I checked the Teletext on the
TV. Blimey, they had all come in! My total winnings:
£800. Linda and I loved it up in Scotland, and spent
every penny of my winnings. We loved being
surrounded by mountains and rivers; the scenery is
truly breathtaking. You can relax and totally chill out.
We went there a number of times, always to different
places: Fort William, Ben Nevis, Grantown-on-Spey, Isle
of Skye, Inverness, The Trossachs and Loch Lomond
being just a few. I recommend it to anyone.

But with the cable work drying up, I had less excuses to be out of Hartlepool, meaning that that naughty lad Trouble started popping his head up again. Not long after returning from a break up in Scotland, I was in a club where one of my old boxing pals, Andy Tucker, was working the door. We were having a good natter about the old days when this geezer comes squaring up to me in a boxer's stance and starts flicking out punches. Both Andy and I knew this nutter, so I told him to pack it in. Now he should have stopped then and everything would have been hunky-dory, but he just wouldn't listen. I had a quick scan of the place and saw that a lot of people were watching; I started to feel embarrassed, as he was still flicking out the jab. Well, wherever there's a crowd ... I casually put my drink on the bar and proceeded to carry out a demolition job on the guy, duly flattening him with a road roller of a punch. I apologised to Andy and left. Another night spoiled over a dickhead being clever.

A few weeks later, I bumped into the prick's older brother, who I knew as a fellow trainer of amateur boxers. He said, 'What the hell did you do that to our kid for?' I told him what had happened, which was different from what he had heard. He knew his brother could be a nuisance when he'd had a drink. He also added that his brother's jaw was broken in two places and it was wired up. So it's only rarely that I get down the town now – there's too much hassle and it's not worth it. I've been there, done it all, bought and worn the T-shirt, and I've now hung it up – still, I haven't washed the blood off yet!

Yet you cannot delete a reputation like mine too easily. It will always create its own trouble. One afternoon, I got a phone call from a friend who wanted to see me. I met up with him and he told me that a few thieves he knew had got caught nicking scrap from a yard by the owner, who shouted to them that 'Richy Horsley will be round to punch your heads in.' This had happened a number of times, so my pal and I went round to see him. I never even knew the guy. When I asked him why he used my name, he just denied it, until I told him to stop taking the piss, whereat he claimed he'd only used it the once. But I knew he was bullshitting me, and informed him that I would be charging for the use of my name. I gave him 24 hours to get what was owed to me.

As we were leaving the yard, my mate gave him the back of his hand.

It turned out that the bloke was so beside himself with worry that he phoned the police. They were planning an ambush, but luckily someone I knew overheard the plotting and phoned me to warn me off. So we never turned up as we were supposed to. Within the hour, though, the police had burst into my pal's house and locked him up for assault. He was told he was looking at some jail. I got a phone call from his brother warning me to be on my toes, so I made a hasty retreat.

Fortunately, someone who knew the scrapman very well went to see him and promised him he would be left alone if he dropped the charges. When the scrapman phoned the policy accordingly, they tried to persuade him not to drop the charges, but they couldn't change his mind, so my friend was released. The scrapman was left alone, as promised. What a fucking carry on though! Saying that, I think everyone involved learned a lesson.

The main stability in my life remained the boxing. Kevin Bennett and Ian Cooper had hung up their amateur vests and turned professional. Neil Fannan took out a trainer's licence, and I was asked if I wanted one too, which of course I did. I had to go to a meeting of the Northern Area Boxing Board of Control and answer questions put to me by members. The former British heavyweight title challenger, Dave Garside, spoke up for me. I had to wait outside the room for five minutes before being called back in. I was told that my application had been successful.

The local paper came out and took some photos of Neil, Benny, Cooper and me. They featured a piece on the back page about the 'New Stable'. At that time, Dave Garside got his promoter's licence and was putting his first show on at the Tall Trees Centre in Yarm. It would be the lads' debut pro fights. The show was a complete sell-out, and everyone involved was a bit nervy. Luckily we watched the Eddie Murphy film *The Nutty Professor* on the TV before the fight, which got rid of any nervous tension. Neil hadn't seen it before and was laughing so much that he was slavering all over the place. Both Benny and Cooper won their fights impressively. On the same bill was a very historical fight between Jan Wild of Stockton and Audrey Guthrie of Newcastle. What was historical about it? It was the very first time that two English female professional boxers had fought each other. Every other pro fight up to then had involved a British woman against a foreign opponent. I worked in Wild's corner handing up – meaning I was in charge of the water bottle and the spit bucket. She won a close decision even though I did think Guthrie deserved it.

I was the resident house second for about five of Dave Garside's shows, all of which took place on a Sunday afternoon. At one show, the two guests of honour were Ernie Shavers, who I have told you about, and Brian London, who fought twice for the same title, losing to Floyd Patterson and Muhammad Ali respectively. Brian was originally a Hartlepool lad but moved to Blackpool when he was young. His father, Jack London, was from Hartlepool and was British Heavyweight Champion in the 1940s. When I think about why Hartlepool has produced so many hard men, I always come to the conclusion that it is down to its history. The town used to be known as 'Little Chicago' because of the amount of gangs it once had. There was the Captain Cutlass Gang, the Turquoise Gang, the Black Hands and loads more. Lots of tough foreign merchant seamen would stay in Hartlepool because it was a thriving seaport, and would spend their cash in a row of pubs called 'The Barbary Coast'.

Just after Kevin Bennett turned professional, we went to Milton Keynes to do a bit of graft. It was an extremely bitter cold December and, to make matters worse, we were working outside. It was proper brass-monkey weather. Whenever we arrived back at the flat, the first one through the door would put the bath straight on, while the others waited their turn and thawed out with a hot cuppa. One night Benny decided to go out jogging and to have a bath when he got back. It was fucking cold outside, and he looked pissed off when he returned. But he was even more pissed off when he found out that all the hot water had gone. Was that the end of it? No, I'm afraid it wasn't. He went into the kitchen to make the dinner that he had been really looking forward to. I was sat at the kitchen table tucking into a large plate of pasta with baked potatoes smothered in butter with a nice cuppa. Lovely. The aroma emanating from my meal was fantastic and it tasted even better, I can tell you. Anyway, Benny opens the fridge and goes for his meal but he can't find it. Where the fuck is it? He asked, 'Richy, have you seen my scran?'

'No mate,' I replied. Benny then eyed me suspiciously and looked at my plate – the food on it looked remarkably like his. I was eating his fucking scran! I had taken the wrong meal out of the fridge, you see. Benny was not amused. All that was left in the fridge was a scabby little shrivelled-up potato with a mangy bit of butter. I tried to explain to him that it was for his own good to keep the fire in his belly, eye of the tiger and all that, but he was having none of it and was in a foul mood all night. But who can blame him? He still thinks I did it on purpose.

My status as a boxing trainer was soon to come to an end though, as my past began to haunt me once more. Some time before I had been featured in a book called *Street Fighters*. The first story in the book is a short rundown about some of my street fights. When there was a story about me in the local paper talking about some of the brutal street fights I've been in and about the forthcoming book, the local Boxing Board asked me to go in for an interview about the *Street Fighting*. I didn't want to sit in front of a bunch of people while they put me on trial – I didn't see what business of theirs it was – so I packed the corner work in.

The publication of the book reinvigorated interest in my street-fighting credentials, and not long after I was contacted by a man who wanted me to have a bare-knuckle fight. I was guaranteed five grand, but the man I would be fighting was a former heavyweight boxer. We had a long talk and everything seemed kosher. I said I needed eight weeks preparation, which he agreed to. I had become so lazy and was moving slower, so I thought this would get my arse in gear. I got weighed and was 19st 12lb. I wrote a training diary so I could keep tabs with what I'd done. Some of you might find it interesting and some might not, but I'm putting it in all the same.

TUESDAY

Went to the beach and walked down to the water's edge and sucked in all that fresh sea air. I start to jog for a couple of minutes and it doesn't take long for me to start sweating. My legs become heavy. I walk for about five mins then jog for another couple. My heart, legs and lungs don't know what's hit them as I get back to the car soaked in sweat.

THURSDAY

Done the same as I did on Tuesday. I've decided I'm going to jog twice a week (Tue & Thur).

TUESDAY

Back to the beach. There were a lot of people with their dogs and I hate jogging past people looking like Mr Blobby so I went to the local athletics track and pushed myself round it three times. It's a quarter of a mile round and I felt like stopping after one lap. It's hard going when you're unfit and this heavy.

Same again, three times round the running track and felt like stopping after once. Some old women were walking their dogs but I wasn't attacked by any of the mutts – that's a first. I think dogs see me as a threat when I run towards them because they usually attack me but not these nice doggies. Went to see an old pal of mine and he said I can train in his gym any time, so I'm going down tomorrow.

FRIDAY

Went to John's gym. He has one room for sparring and grappling, another is filled with free weights and a weights machine and the other is filled with kick bags and punch bags. He also has an office; it's a really nice set-up. I've known John for twenty years and training is his life. He is a great instructor, conditioner and motivator; a good man to have in your corner is John. He's a black belt fourth Dan in one style of fighting, fifth Dan in another and also the highest grade you can get in kick boxing and runs his own academy. A great guy, only small but not to be messed with. He could smash about six bones in your body before you could say Peking Duck. Anyway, I done a round of skipping and had a bit of a lather on because it doesn't half get you warmed up. Charlie P took me on the pads for two rounds and that was enough for me – I felt like spewing.

MONDAY

One round skipping and three on the pads with John. I felt like I needed oxygen after that, John makes you work so hard.

TUESDAY

Three times round the running track. I like to do my running early so the air is as clean as possible.

WEDNESDAY

One round skipping. One light round on bag. Three rounds on pads with John. He never lets you settle and makes you work every second of every round.

THURSDAY

Three times round the running track.

FRIDAY

Three rounds skipping. Got a good sweat on and then done three rounds on the pads working on speed. It was all speed, speed, speed and I couldn't breathe; it was intense. The gym was hot and humid and I drank plenty of fluids.

MONDAY

Two skipping. One heavy bag. Three on the pads again working on speed. When I got home I had a nice hot bath and felt great. I got a buzz I'd never had in years and it felt really good. Also every three days I've been doing 120 press-ups (3 sets of 40).

TUESDAY

Four times round the running track. I pushed myself to do an extra one and felt great after a bath. I can feel a big change in my body and it feels 100% better. Not bad for a fat bastard.

WEDNESDAY

One round shadow boxing. Two rounds skipping. Three rounds on the heavy bag.

THURSDAY

Four times round the running track again. I'm over the moon with myself. I'm gonna stick to four times round twice a week, that's enough for me.

FRIDAY

Finished the week with a good session. Done some stretching and then three skipping. One shadow boxing. Two on the pads working on speed and finished off with two on the bag. I'm hitting a lot harder and getting a lot faster. Starting to buzz.

MONDAY

Two skipping. One shadow. Two pads. Two bag. Finished off with legs on weight machine.

TUESDAY

Four times round running track. 120 press-ups. Got weighed and was bang on 19 stone.

WEDNESDAY

Stretching. One shadow. Two skipping. One bag. Three pads. Finished with legs on weight machine.

THURSDAY

Woke up this morning with a trapped nerve at the bottom of my neck, right in between the shoulder blades. It's the exact same nerve that's been trapped twice before and had to be freed both times by a chiropractor as I was in agony. I still ran round the track four times but I was in pain.

FRIDAY

I've been awake most of the night with jolts of

pain every time I move. I can't go to the gym like this so I'm going for a massage.

MONDAY

Trapped nerve has knocked hell out of me all weekend. I had a couple of massages but they were only good for a short time. I've had a session with a chiropractor and it feels much better. £30 for the first time and £25 every time after that. I was told to do certain exercises in the hope that it might free itself. It has to get better soon as I need to be training.

WEDNESDAY

Just back from chiropractors and it feels 100% better.

THURSDAY

Four times round the running track. 120 press-ups. Trapped nerve has been released. Cushty.

FRIDAY

Back in the gym after a week. One round shadow. One round skipping. Three rounds on the pads. Felt OK. The break might have done me a bit of good even though you wouldn't think it. I'll give you an example here. When my mate fought for (and won) the British title years ago they had twelve weeks of training mapped out, as it was over fifteen rounds back then. After six weeks he felt like he was peaking and the people looking after him gave him a week off the gym but he still done his morning run. It kept him from going stale. He felt fresh again when he went back to the gym and done the last five weeks and peaked at the right time and won the title in the fourteenth round.

SATURDAY

120 press-ups.

MONDAY

Two skipping. Two shadow. Three bag. Legs on weight machine.

TUESDAY

Four times round the running track. 120 press-ups.

WEDNESDAY

Stretching. One skipping. Two heavy bag. Three pads.

THURSDAY

Four times round the running track. 120 press-ups.

FRIDAY

Two shadow. Two skipping. Two heavy bag. Two pads. Legs on machine.

MONDAY

Two shadow. Three skipping. Four heavy bag. Legs on machine.

TUESDAY

Four times round the running track. 120 press-ups.

Later that day, I got a phone call to say that the fight was off. The geezer had pulled out. I wasn't given an explanation. I couldn't believe it. All that training for nothing – it would be an understatement if I said I wasn't too pleased. All I got was an embarrassing apology. At the time I was fuming but, thinking about it now, it was probably for the best.

After all, in the grand scheme of things this was just a minor issue. I realised this most strongly one morning in July 2001, when our Debbie's fella came walking up to my door and told me that my sister Jackie was dead. It took the wind right out of my sails. I asked what happened and he replied, 'She killed herself.' I couldn't get my head round that: Jacqueline wouldn't kill herself, she had six children at home and they were her life – she doted on them. I said I was going straight round to see Debra but he said she was visiting family and wouldn't be back until two o'clock. When I did get round there I was in a complete daze. Debra was in the kitchen making a cup of tea and her eyes were red and bloodshot with crying. I was also choked up with red eyes. Debra started telling me about what had been going on.

She said Jackie had phoned her a few hours before she died. Jackie said that her oldest son Andrew, who she hadn't seen for years, had turned up out of the blue a couple of weeks before. He was eating her out of house and home and wasn't giving her a penny. She said to Debra that he was a stranger and was thinking about asking him to leave, but was worried what people would think. She had been married to Paul and then got divorced, but they were still together, although he wasn't living with her. It turned out that she and Paul hadn't been getting on and he was being very difficult. That afternoon, she went to a pub to see him and found him all over a woman. An argument erupted and she stormed off.

When she phoned Debra at 9.45pm, she told her what had been going on and after a few minutes said, 'I'll have to go because I'm going out.' Debbie enquired, 'This late?' Jackie said, 'I'll phone you tomorrow,' and finished the conversation. Those were the very last words they ever spoke. We don't entirely know what happened afterwards. Paul and Andrew are the only ones who know what really happened; Andrew was having nightmares for weeks after.

Paul said Jackie went upstairs and they could hear her walking about. He said that she sat on the bedroom floor and had a cigarette. Then she wrapped the lead from the vacuum cleaner around her neck tightly, about nine times, and passed out through lack of oxygen to the brain. When he went upstairs, he struggled to get the door open as she was laid against it. He spotted the lead around her neck as soon as he got in. He said her eyes were vacant and he knew she was gone. The ambulance came and found a faint pulse and gave her the electric-shock treatment, but couldn't bring her back. That was at 1.30am. At 2am, she was pronounced dead. She was only 38 years old.

Paul said there wasn't a suicide note. If Jackie had planned to kill herself she would have definitely left a note. The six children were asleep in the other bedrooms. The post mortem said the cause of death was strangulation by ligature and at the inquest there was an open verdict. I went with Debbie to the hospital morgue to identify Jackie, and the marks on her neck were visible. We were shocked to see our sister like that. Deb and I did some running around sorting the funeral out. The day before the funeral, I had one hour alone with her and was talking to her and crying my eyes out. She looked beautiful, just like sleeping beauty. The morning of the funeral, I had another hour alone with her. I wanted to say goodbye to my sister in private, as it was very personal to me.

There is a turquoise stone that is sacred to the American Indian and I put one in her sleeve and kissed her. The funeral was very emotional and I still haven't got over her death. There's not a day goes by that I don't think of her. She smiles at me every day from a picture I have of her on my wall. Westlife were her favourite band and we played two of their records at her funeral. I have a lock of her hair, which I value as my most prized possession. It can never be replaced. I still have a little soft spot for her daughter Stacey, as I looked after her for a short time when she was a baby. Paul is looking after all the children now with the help of his family. It is all very sad.

Two months after Jackie passed away, my mam's second husband Ken died. He'd been in a home for a few years and died of natural causes. Soon after, the adopted daughter of my mam's friend, Annie Bobbin, died of kidney failure. Joanne was buried on Christmas Eve. She left an eight-year-old daughter, who is now being brought up by her grandparents. There was another friend of mine who died around the same time, who choked on her vomit. She was the same age as Joanne, both only 25 years old. You can be talking to someone one minute and they'll be gone the next. Life is so short; you have to make the most of it while you can because we are not here on this earth very long. Needless to say, all this anguish put my own problems firmly into perspective.

As I started losing family and friends, I was moved to try and find out more about my own ancestry. I heard of a good medium called Peter Crawford who lived in a town not too far from me. I had a private sitting with him and what he told me was unreal. He was spot-on with everything and everyone. I got messages from my dad, Granny Horsley, my sister Jackie and my pal H. He said Gran was with her sister Margaret, who had died when only a child. He also told me he could see horse-drawn gypsy trailers in a field and horses grazing and gypsy men sat round a campfire talking. He said if I checked it out I would find that I had gypsy blood in me and that these spirits were my family from generations ago. This corresponded with a similar message I have already told you that I had years before. When I told my sister Debra, she said that she thought there was a gypsy link somewhere. She was sure she'd heard something like that when she was a child but couldn't be sure.

A few days later, she phoned me and said, 'I've just been talking to my mother on the phone and I asked her if there was any gypsy blood in the family.' She had said that her mother – my biological grandmother – was a pure-bred Romany gypsy who had been brought up in a children's orphanage in Leeds; her name was Ellen Hopkins. Debra went on, 'She doesn't know how old she was when she went in or what happened to her parents. We don't know if her name was already Hopkins or whether the orphanage gave her it. She died some years ago.' That was a bit of a shock to me, but there you have it – I do have gypsy blood in me.

I have a good friend called Louis Welch, who is a Romany gypsy. The late Bartley Gorman, in his autobiography *King Of The Gypsies*, rated Louis as one of the best bare-knuckle fighters in the British Isles. One day, when he was at my house, I told Louis the story of my gypsy blood and he was a little surprised and then said, 'We could be related.' Then he told me something which really surprised me. He said that he was born in Hartlepool, at Cameron Hospital. I was shocked, especially as I was born in the same hospital. We came into this world on the same spot, probably only feet apart.

I had certainly had enough fights to qualify as a true-blood gypsy. But when the medium repeated that I was very lucky to have not killed someone, I decided never to fight on the streets again. If those messages aren't warnings for me to stop then I don't know what is. Only a matter of a few years ago, a lad was killed in our town with one punch. You don't only ruin your life, but you ruin your family's life, and that of the victim and the victim's family. It's not worth it.

My own health was taking a bit of a bashing even without the fighting. I developed a hernia just above my belly button, known as an umbilical hernia. It develops when the intestine pushes through the stomach wall. I don't know how I got it but it kept getting bigger and eventually looked like a golf ball. I was referred to the hospital and was told straight away that it needed surgery. I wanted to lose a little bit of weight before I went in, so I shed a stone. I went in hospital on the Sunday, had the operation on the Monday and was released by Tuesday teatime. They had cut me open, and pushed the intestine back in before putting a mesh gauze there so it couldn't push back through. I had to take it easy until it healed up, but I'm OK now. I've taken a few good shots in the gym in my belly and had the medicine ball smacked off it loads of times and it's fine.

As my interest in fighting began to wane, I started to get into birds – no, not the lasses, but birds of prey. I went to a bird-of-prey centre with Tommy and George and had a good look round. We started talking to the blokes who ran the place; they would kindly give advice and answer questions. There was a flying display on at the time, and the birds would swoop down and fly just above your head and put the shits up you. One of the blokes gave me the glove to put on and part of a baby chick as food, which I placed on one of my gloved fingers. He gave a signal and this big buzzard came flying out of the trees and swooped down on to my fist and took the chick. The power of those birds is unreal. We were there about three hours and had a great time. What was significant about it was as soon as I got home, I put the TV on and all the stations were live to America because the World Trade Centre was on fire after a hijacked plane had crashed into one of the towers. Then I watched as the second plane went into the other tower. I couldn't believe what I was seeing and the rest is history. I'll never forget what I was doing on September 11.

I had an aviary built, and filled it with all sorts of birds, Canaries, Cutthroats, Silver Bills, Strawberry Finches, and so on. They bred like wildfire. I never sold any of the young, preferring to give them away for free. I bred for pleasure, not profit. I did that for over two years and enjoyed it, but then I decided to have a break and gave the birds to my friend who has a pet shop.

I cleaned out the aviary and it was stood empty for about six months. One day Tommy said, 'You know what would look well in that aviary?'

'What?' I asked.

'An owl,' he replied.

I'd never given a thought to owning an owl before but he planted the seed and it seemed like a good idea. I bought a book and a video on owls before so I could understand them a bit more. I had a look in the local ad-mag and found an ad for a young eight-month-old Barn Owl for sale. I eagerly phoned up; it hadn't been sold. It was at a place called Seaton Delaval, which was about fifty miles up the North East coastline. I had been there about 12 years before to see a Scottish medium called Mary Duffy give an evening of clairvoyance to a packed hall. When we arrived at the house the guy who opened the door looked like a New Age traveller. Out the back, he had aviaries with birds of prey in. He knew what he was talking about and he handled the birds with majestic ease. He showed us the owl, which was a beauty. He was feeding him on baby chicks and he gave me some to take home. I also used to give him mice once a week as well for a change. I would watch him at night to see his actions because my aviary was situated in an open space and surrounded by trees and birds – it was like being in the wild for him.

I started a new trend because not much later Tommy bought a pair of European Eagle Owls. George, who I call Bald Eagle, bought a pair of Turk Owls. Mick Burns bought a pair of African Spotted Eagle Owls and Maori bought a pair of Snowy Owls. I called my owl Barney because he was a Barn Owl. I had him for a year. When the mating season started, he was calling all night for a mate – I couldn't get to sleep so I decided that he had to go, but I wanted a good home for him, so gave him to a friend of Mick Burns called Gerry. He was a great bloke and a proper naturalist and a little eccentric. He keeps Barney in a lovely aviary and he's well looked after.

Gerry had had a few run-ins with the law when he was a young man, and had been known by the nickname 'Screw' Lawson, as he chinned a few coppers in his time. But with age he had mellowed out, and become an authority on wildlife in general. He is 66 now and still active with his dogs. He moved to the Shires and lived in an isolated cottage on his own for 12 years, hunting and studying wildlife while working in the kitchens at the Military College, in Wiltshire. He returned to the North East a few years ago and settled in Hartlepool for about 18 months before moving up to Shotton.

CHAPTER 20

THE LONDON RETURN OF CRAZY HORSE

After hearing of my sister's tragic death, the infamous prisoner Charles Bronson sent me a very nice letter of condolence. We exchanged a few letters after that, and he even wrote a tribute to me for inclusion in this book. Not long after, I was invited as a guest to one of his art shows being held on his behalf somewhere in Yorkshire. To cut a long story short, I never turned up and about a week later I received a nasty letter from Bronson demanding a reason for my non-show. A line from the letter reads: 'Is that your fucking game, disrespecting people?' Bronson then contacted a friend of mine called Terry in London, requesting a fight with me as soon as he got released from prison on parole. In spite of my temporary retirement from fighting, you have to admit it was an offer I couldn't refuse. But will Bronson ever be released? I've got my fingers crossed in hope that the fight does happen; it'll be a nice littler earner and I'm certain I'll be victorious. So watch this space.

In the meantime, Tony suggested I take a few unlicensed fights to get fit and shake off the ring rust. This was a timely suggestion as I had been out of the ring for 14 years – my last amateur fight was way back in 1989. I was well out of shape and weighing in at a gigantic twenty stone. Over the next couple of weeks, I gave it some serious thought. I was almost 39. Was I too old for it? I knew that my best fighting days were behind me, but this was probably my last shot at the big time. I also knew that in years to come I'd be sitting by the fire with my pipe and slippers thinking about the opportunity that I had let slip through my fingers. The answer had to be: Yes, bring it on!

Now I had to go on a diet as well as start training. I needed the right fuel in my body, as the slightest disadvantage can be the difference between glory and defeat. My diet routine was the following: Breakfast: bowl of Cornflakes or Rice Krispies, with only a sweetener – no sugar allowed. Sometimes I'd also have 4 soft-boiled eggs. Mid-morning: a banana and an apple. Lunch: baked potato with tuna or beans. Mid-afternoon: two pieces of fruit. Dinner: steak or chicken or fish or pasta, with a choice of three vegetables. Evening meal: one piece of fruit, and a tea or coffee with sweeteners. I could drink as much fruit juice and water as I liked. I stuck to the diet and never once wavered – the stakes were too fucking high. And it worked: on 14 May 2004, I had weighed 20st 2lb, but on the day of the fight eight weeks later I weighed 18st dead – a loss of 30lb!

The diet was only one aspect of the training, as of course I had to put some serious work in, in the gym. After all, I was going to be fighting in front of 2,000 people so I didn't want to make a fool of myself. I also kept a diary of my training so I could look back at it and know exactly what I'd done right or wrong. When you do this, you know whether or not you've put the work in. If you don't put the work in, you are only fooling yourself because if you cut corners there is always a price to pay. I'll put my training diary in so you can see how I built my fitness up.

WEDNESDAY 14 MAY

3x2 mins skipping.

THURSDAY 15 MAY

3x1 min on pads.

SATURDAY 17 MAY

3x2 mins skipping.

TUESDAY 20 MAY

2x2 min skipping. 2x2 min punch bag.

THURSDAY 22 MAY

3x1 min on pads.

FRIDAY 23 MAY

3x2 min skipping.

SATURDAY 24 MAY

Three shadow boxing. Thee skipping. Later that day, I agreed to fight Tony 'Rock Hard' Louis on 17 July at the Hammersmith Palais, in London.

TUESDAY 27 MAY

Three pads. Two punch bag.

WEDNESDAY 28 MAY

Three shadow boxing. Three skipping.

THURSDAY 29 MAY

Three pads. Two punch bag.

FRIDAY 30 MAY

One shadow boxing. Four skipping.

SATURDAY 31 MAY

Three shadow boxing. Three skipping.

MONDAY 2 JUNE

Jogging. Four times round sports track.

TUESDAY 3 JUNE

Three pads. Five bag.

WEDNESDAY 4 JUNE

Jogging. Four times round track.

THURSDAY 5 JUNE

Three pads. Six bag.

FRIDAY 6 JUNE

Jogging. Four times round track.

SUNDAY 8 JUNE

Three skipping.

MONDAY 9 JUNE

Jogging. Four times round track.

TUESDAY 10 JUNE

Two skipping. Three pads.

WEDNESDAY 11 JUNE

Jogging. Five times round track.

THURSDAY 12 JUNE

Three pads. Six bag.

FRIDAY 13 JUNE

Jogging. Five times round track.

SATURDAY 14 JUNE
Four sparring. Five bag.

MONDAY 16 JUNE
Jogging. Five times round track.

TUESDAY 17 JUNE
Three pads. Three sparring.

WEDNESDAY 18 JUNE
am. Jogging. Five times round track. pm. Two skipping. Four sparring. Three bag.

THURSDAY 19 JUNE
Three pads. Five bag.

FRIDAY 20 JUNE
Jogging. Five times round track.

SATURDAY 21 JUNE
Three sparring.

MONDAY 23 JUNE
Jogging. Six times round track.

TUESDAY 24 JUNE
Three pads. Eight bag.

WEDNESDAY 25 JUNE

am. Jogging. Six times round track. pm. Four skipping. Four sparring. Four bag. Two pads.

THURSDAY 26 JUNE

Three pads. Twelve bag.

FRIDAY 27 JUNE

Jogging. Six times round track.

MONDAY 30 JUNE

Six times round track.

TUESDAY 1 JULY

Three pads. Ten bag.

WEDNESDAY 2 JULY

Jogging. Six times round track.

THURSDAY 3 JULY

Three pads. Twelve bag.

FRIDAY 4 JULY

Jogging. Six times round track.

SUNDAY 6 JULY

Three pads.

MONDAY 7 JULY

am. Jogging. Six times round track. pm. Five sparring. Six bag.

TUESDAY 8 JULY

Thirteen skipping.

WEDNESDAY 9 JULY

Jogging. Six times round track.

THURSDAY 10 JULY

Two skipping. Three pads. Three bag.

FRIDAY 11 JULY

Jogging. Six times round track.

SATURDAY 12 JULY

Five skipping. Three bag. Three pads. Twenty mins bike.

SUNDAY 13 JULY

Three pads.

MONDAY 14 JULY

am. Jogging. Six times round track. pm. Five pads.

As you can see, I worked hard for this fight and made sacrifices. Once or twice, as I was going home from a session in the gym, I felt like saying, Fuck it, this is too hard, but I hung in there and stayed with it. I had some excellent sparring sessions with 'Big Shanny'. He is 6ft 2in tall and weighs in at 16 stone, is as fit as a lop and often goes out on 10-mile runs. He's a really good heavyweight boxer and as strong as a bull. He put me through it in sparring and got me prepared. He brought me on no end and I can't thank him enough. As well as Big Shanny, I would like to thank Craig and Mark Denton for some first-class sparring. Mark is No 2 Amateur Middleweight in England and has a tattoo on his back that says, 'Pain is temporary, pride is forever.' Also, thanks to John Dawson for giving me some excellent conditioning work.

I did all the homework on my opponent Tony 'Rock Hard' Louis. He had had around forty fights and then retired for about six years, making a comeback only a few years ago in the unlicensed ring, having fifteen more fights. He was certainly no mug. I got hold of a couple of his fights on video so I could have a good look at him. He was a very clever fighter with a good defence, and hardly ever got caught by punches to the head. Going for his head and hitting nothing but gloves and arms will tire you out very quickly, so I devised a plan to attack the body to force his arms down. I accordingly worked on my body shots in training.

I went to London with John, one of my trainers. We met up with my other man, Biff, on the day of the fight.

We stayed with old friends, Steve and Sofia, who made us very welcome. Steve was a former Hartlepool lad who I'd known since the 1970s. We stayed for three days in all. It was a great place to find peace and just relax and get focused about the job ahead. But as the fight time drew nearer, the butterflies inevitably got stronger. All the training and homework was done; it was all down to me now to deliver and produce the goods on the day itself.

We went to the Hammersmith Palais by taxi. All the way there, John and Biff were talking to me from the back seat, psyching me up. The place was packed out when we arrived. The bouncers on the door were huge and I was recognised straight away because my picture was on all the posters for the show. I was to be fighting the last bout of the night – the top of the bill. Inside the venue, there were well-known celebrities from TV and film: top professional boxers, gypsy fighters, glamour models, well-known football hooligans, bare-knuckle fighters, underworld gangsters and even one of the great train robbers, Bruce Reynolds, was at the ringside. They had all come to see this guy, Crazy Horse! When we got into the dressing room, it was like a blast furnace. There was no air to breathe and everyone was sweating cobs. As all the celebrities were in the ring auctioning things, I slipped outside and grabbed a bit of fresh air. It was beautiful as it cooled me down and allowed me to look up to the sky and get some focus. I went back in after 15 minutes, and was gloved up. Then the music started blaring and I knew my opponent was on his way to the ring.

Halfway through the record, the music stopped and the MC announced a five-minute delay. It didn't take a genius to work out they were playing the waiting game to unnerve me. I paced up and down in the waiting area for five minutes like a caged tiger, preparing myself mentally. Then the MC announced, 'Tony "Rock Hard" Louis,' and his music came on. This time I knew it was for real.

The music eventually faded. Now it was my turn to be introduced. The MC's voice boomed out and announced that I was the opponent 'from Hartlepool'. A big cheer went up and the roof nearly came off with the noise from all my supporters. I made my way through the crowd to the booming and deafening beat of Queen's 'We Will Rock You'. I was getting slaps on the back as I went through the crowd. People were screaming my name. But I was too focused to take any notice. When I eventually climbed into the ring I knew that this would be my night. Nothing would stop me from claiming the winner's trophy. I was willing myself to win so much so that I didn't even hear the MC announce my opponent. The first time I heard anything was when he reannounced my name, introducing me as 'the street-fighting champion himself'.

Now I was confident, but don't get me wrong: I

respected my high-profile opponent, as I never underestimate anybody. It especially takes a special breed of man to climb through those ropes and step into the ring in front of a crowd of people all baying for blood. Nothing has changed since the days of the Romans. It was proper gladiatorial stuff.

The referee called us to the centre of the ring. I stood face to face with my opponent for the first time. I hardly heard a word the ref said as I fixed my gaze upon Tony 'Rock Hard' Louis. We touched gloves, a sporting gesture, and then went back to our corners. Time for war. The bell sounded.

I went straight for him and slammed in a hard right to the body, but he covered up nicely. He was very fast for a 17-stone fighter, so I cut the ring size down, as I didn't want to waste essential energy chasing him. I gradually walked him down. I started slamming lefts and rights into his body to bring his hands down, just as planned. I added a powerful right jab for good measure.

He was throwing jabs back, but I was so single-minded that I brushed them aside like confetti and walked through them. Then he loaded up with a big right which caught me flush on the nose: BANG! The sweat sprayed from my head. I wasn't hurt, but I was narked with myself for getting caught. Luckily though it only made me more focused to end the fight.

I exploded into action. I bullied him into his corner. A right hook to the body, but he covered well. Another mighty hook to the body, but still his hands didn't drop. I changed tack, and threw a feigned punch, a right uppercut, then switched to the left and whipped in an atomic iron left hook into his ribs. CRACK! He went down, unable to hide the feeling of agony on his face. The pain was too much for him. He spat out his gum shield, and tried to catch his breath. I had robbed him of his wind.

The referee started counting. When he reached five, Tony 'Rock Hard' Louis, lying on the canvas on his back, shook his head to say he wasn't getting back up. When the ref said 'Ten', my supporters went wild. The fight had lasted a total of one minute and thirty seconds, yet it had felt like an eternity.

It would be a massive understatement to say I got a great feeling from the victory. I had done the business in the capital, in front of a large crowd. As I left the ring to head back to the dressing room, I was literally mobbed, with well-wishers patting me on the back. People who had come to support me were overcome with emotion. Everyone wanted to hug me and have photos taken with me – I felt more like a pop star than a fighter. It was certainly something else. Afterwards, my opponent came up to me and said that the left hook I landed to his body was the hardest body shot he'd ever been hit by.

When I arrived home the next day, everyone was still buzzing. I didn't know it, but on the night of the fight there were about eight people at my mam's having a drink and waiting for a phone call about the result. Our Joanne's husband had given them a running commentary over the phone. When the fight was over, some of them were dancing and singing in the front garden, shedding tears of joy. The neighbours must have thought they were mad. But what is more, I know my dad, Tommy, was looking down and smiling, as proud as punch of his boy.

CHAPTER 21

UNFINISHED BUSINESS

After my victory at the Warriors 1, the self-proclaimed and well-named 'Monarch of the Underworld', Dave Courtney, came up to me. He commended me when he said, 'Richy, you can hit. I'm fucking glad you're not hitting me.' He said it in such a way and with this expression on his face that he made me laugh. He is now a good friend of mine, although due to distance I don't see that much of him these days. Sometimes people misunderstood him, but the man has always been all right with me. We get on particularly well due to having the same dry sense of humour. Not long after my win, Dave called me up out of the blue and asked me whether I wanted to help out with a situation. Tony Lambrianou, a former Kray henchman, had died of a suspected heart attack, and Dave was in charge of security at the funeral.

Because it was a former Kray henchman, there were rumours that trouble was brewing, and that something was going to kick-off at the funeral. Dave asked me to help make sure everything would pass off smoothly.

The following morning, Dave and I paid a few visits to some unsavoury characters, all of whom shall remain nameless. They were firmly told them they were not welcome at the funeral service and to stay away, if they knew what was good for them. But we didn't just leave it at that; we wanted to be sure, so we knocked seven colours of shit out of them. They got the message and the funeral of Tony Lambrianou went ahead without a hitch. I didn't even need to attend the service, as we had made sure everything would go without at hitch. Now that was a favour for Dave Courtney, not the Kray name.

When I look back, I sometimes wish I had stuck at school and got myself a good job, but the cards just were dealt to me like that! I also wish that I had gone into the ring 100% fit. A lot of the time, I was unfit, full of flu, overweight and even once with a hangover. I think the only things that got me through times like that were my ability to take a punch and my lion heart.

I've spent a lot of time reflecting on my life, and I'm trying to become a better person. I'm thinking about going to college to study – I'm not sure which subject yet, but something I enjoy. They always say that it's never too late, don't they … I might just take them up on the offer.

BOXING CORNER

Here is a profile of some local boxers, old and new, a number of whom I have fought. You will already know some of the characters I've mentioned from the book, but I thought that a little background would add another dimension. But remember that these are not definitive career profiles as such. I have added details from memory, but naturally I can't remember every aspect to their careers.

TERRY ALLEN ALIAS DAVE ALLEN
D.O.B. 24-5-59
Bantamweight
Fights:9 Won: 0 Lost: 9.
You got to take your hat off to the guy for having a go.

SEAN ARMSTRONG
D.O.B. 22-9-68
Welterweight.
Fights: 3 Won: 2 Lost: 1

'Biff' fought Shea Neary in Liverpool on his debut. Totally dedicated to boxing but always suffered with bad hands which cut short his career and has had numerous operations on them.

CRAWFORD ASHLEY
D.O.B. 20-5-64
Fights: 44 Won: 33 Lost: 10 Drew: 1

I boxed Crawford in the 1981 Junior ABAs. He won six National titles as a junior and was a devastating puncher who could take you out with either hand. As a pro he became British Champion, and won a Lonsdale Belt outright. He also won the European title and had a couple of World title fights.

KEVIN BENNETT
D.O.B. 15-8-75
Fights: 21 Won: 7 Lost: 4

As an amateur Benny was always the bridesmaid and never the bride. An England International who won a bronze medal in the multi-nations, and was a runner-up in the NABCs and an ABA finalist. I travelled around the country with him in the season before he turned pro and witnessed him receive a number diabolical decisions.

But he never moaned and just got on with it. A close friend who recently became Commonwealth Lightweight title holder as a pro.

BILLY BESSEY
D.O.B. 8-1-74
Super Heavyweight
Fights: 6 Won: 4 Lost: 2
Big Bill was A.B.A Super Heavyweight Champion in 1999. Showed a lot of courage and determination in his title fight win when all looked lost but had the heart of a champion and pulled it out the fire. Moved back to his native Portsmouth and is still active as a pro.

GEORGE BOWES
D.O.B. 1-9-36
Fights: 62 Won: 42 Lost: 16 Drew: 4
George is one of the old school who seems to have been around forever. He has a wealth of experience in the fight game. A top-class amateur who had over sixty fights in a ten-year pro career. He challenged for the British title in 1964 but was stopped on cuts. As a trainer he guided the Feeney brothers to British Championships.

PETER CANTERDALE
D.O.B. 7-7-64

Welterweight

Fights: 6 Won: 5 Lost: 1

I've known Peter about 26 years and also worked the doors with him back in the eighties. He turned pro in 1986 and seven months later retired for good.

MARK CHICHOCKI
D.O.B. 18-10-67

Light Middleweight

Fights: 11 Won: 6 Lost: 5

Chi was a good amateur and also took the Northern Area belt as a pro with a 10th round KO in a great fight back in '93. I should know, I was there!

STEVE CONWAY
D.O.B. 6-10-77

Lightweight

Fights: 37 Won: 31 Lost: 6

Born and Bred in Hartlepool and is a relative of mine through marriage. Already had a shot at British title against Alex Arthur at Featherweight. Steve is a awkward and tricky southpaw who is still very much active. Now resides in Yorkshire.

IAN COOPER
D.O.B. 3-5-74

Fights: 9 Won: 8 Lost: 1

Dubbed Super Cooper, he was a Junior ABA finalist, ABA finalist and then the ABA Champion. He was also an England International. A gifted and skilful boxer who more often than not would like to stand and trade. He won his first eight fights as a pro, including the Northern Area and British Masters titles, before losing on points to a journeyman in a mauling, spoiling fight. Took the loss badly and retired. Eighteen months later, he received four years' imprisonment for GBH. He is a good lad and I hope he can get his life back on track when he's released. He still has a lot to offer boxing and would make a good coach.

MAURICE CULLEN
Born 30-12-37

Lightweight

Fights: 55 Won: 45 Lost: 8 Drew: 2

Maurice was British Champ and won a Lonsdale belt outright. Fought and won at Madison Square Gardens in New York in 1967. Lost to two legendary world champs in Carlos Ortiz and Ken Buchanan and retired in 1970.

DARREN ELSDEN
D.O.B. 16-2-71

Super Featherweight

Fights: 8 Won: 5 Lost: 2 Drew: 1

I remember Darren when he first started boxing at our club when he was knee high to a grasshopper. Won Northern Area title with a 7th round KO. Retired soon after.

NEIL FANNAN
D.O.B. 17-6-59

Fights: 16 Won: 10 Lost: 5 Drew: 1

A good amateur and decent pro at light middle and middleweight. Very tough with a terrific body punch. Now a pro trainer with a few champions under his belt. A disciplinarian who demands 100%.

GEORGE FEENEY
D.O.B. 9-2-57.

Fights: 29 Won: 19 Lost: 10

British Lightweight Champion and winner of a Lonsdale Belt outright. George had a granite chin and bags of stamina, and had a close fight with the World Champ. He retired after an eye operation to repair a detached retina while still British Champ. A really nice bloke who is also a good cut man to have in your corner.

JOHN FEENEY
D.O.B. 15-5-58
Fights: 48 Won: 35 Lost: 13
John won Junior titles as an amateur and was ABA runner-up in 1976. As a pro he was British Bantamweight Champion twice. He had seven British title fights, four European title fights and even fought for the Commonwealth title in the Sydney Opera House.

KEITH FOREMAN
D.O.B. 29-7-62
Super Featherweight
Fights: 36 Won: 13 Lost: 21 Drew: 2
Keith fought the best in Britain. His record reads like a who's who. When I think of Keith and his twin brother ken my nose starts to bleed.

KEN FOREMAN
D.O.B. 29-7-62
Fights: 46 Won: 31 Lost: 15
I first met Ken in 1978 when we boxed for the same club, United Services BC. He had over a hundred amateur fights. A very slick and skilful southpaw, with a jab that was second to none. Ken was a contender as a pro and had a number of televised fights. He was also Northern Area Champ.

TEDDY GARDNER
D.O.B. 21-1-22
Fights: 66 Won: 55 Lost: 8 Drew: 3
Boxed his early career under the name of Teddy Baker.
Teddy was a triple champion at flyweight. In 1952 he
was British, Commonwealth – at that time called the
Empire – and European Champion. When he retired he
ran a pub called 'The Square Ring', which had framed
boxing pictures covering the walls.

DAVE GARSIDE
D.O.B: 14-3-63
Fights: 45 Won: 27 Lost: 18
England International and ABA runner-up in 1981. A
very tough man with the heart of a lion. Dave loved
training and always turned up for fights in great
condition. Challenged for the British title as a pro.
Married to Brian London's daughter. Now a successful
businessman.

PHIL GIBSON
D.O.B.15-1-61
Light Middleweight
Fights: 14 Won: 7 Lost: 6 Drew: 1
N.A.B.C Finalist in 1978. Never stopped as a pro, very
tough and durable was Phil.

EDDIE GLASS
D.O.B. 1-2-56
Featherweight
Fights: 13 Won: 0 Lost: 11 Drew: 2
Poor Eddie never won one. At least he kept getting in and trying. It takes a special breed of man to climb up the steps and through the ropes in front of a crowd who all want to see blood.

MARTIN HARTY
He was tough and durable. I fought him twice back in 1981 and won both. In our second fight, I dropped him in the first round with a lovely punch. He came back at me in the second round and had me rocking and out on my feet. We both had bust noses and black eyes. He also broke his right hand in the fight.

MOHAMMED HELEL
D.O.B. 16-6-74
Welterweight
Fights: 10 Won: 2 Lost: 8
Mo was from Tunisia and reached the national novice final. A very polite man who always had a smile on his face. Last seen working as a waiter in a retaraunt.

JACKIE HORSEMAN
D.O.B. 3-3-21
Featherweight
Fights: 48 Won: 6 Lost: 38 Drew: 4
Jackie was a journey man and would stand in at the last minute for anyone. He had an all-action style which the fans loved and was noted as a promoter's man. Anytime, anyplace, anywhere, that was Jackie. Northern Area champ in 1951 and retired in '56.

CHRIS HUBBERT
D.O.B. 30-5-68
Heavyweight
Fights: 6 Won: 3 Lost: 3
Big Chris 6ft 4in was an excellent Lt-Heavy as an amateur and I recall him winning 22 out of 23 fights in one season. Had a couple of years out and piled the beef on and turned pro as a Heavyweight.

MICHAEL HUNTER
Born 5-5-78
Fights: 22 Won: 21 Lost: 0 Drew: 1
England International. European Junior bronze medallist. NABC title holder. ABA Flyweight Champion. ABA Bantamweight Champion. Undefeated pro who added the WBF Super Bantamweight title to his list of honours. Also Northern Area Champion and British Champion. The better the fighter in front of him, the

better he fights. I'm sure there'll be more titles for
Michael before he's through.

GORDON JACKSON
A heavily built, short southpaw heavyweight from
Sunderland. He came at me like a bullet, looking for a
quick finish. I weathered his early storm and hit him
back in tremendous fashion. It only lasted two minutes
and forty seconds but it was a beauty. I never heard of
him after that: I think I finished him as a fighter.

FRANCIS JONES
D.O.B: 7-2-81
Light Middleweight
Fights: 13 Won: 8 Lost: 2 Drew: 2 No Contest: 1
Franny Rat fought Danny Moir for the vacant Northern
Area belt but during the 3rd round crowd trouble
turned into a riot and the fight was abandoned and
declared a no contest. They are supposed to be meeting
again for the vacant belt, let's hope the crowd are on
their best behaviour.

PAUL KEERS
D.O.B. 22-10-60
Lightweight
Fights 42 Won 14 Lost 25. Drew 3
'Lofty' was a good Featherweight and was on the verge
of a British title eliminator but making the weight was
too much for him and moved up to Lightweight but
found them a bit too big.

JOHN T. KELLY.
D.O.B. 12-6-70
Lightweight
Fights: 58 Won: 26 Lost: 26 Drew: 6
'Corn Dog' Kelly lifted the Northern Area crown but
had to retire less than a year later with eye trouble.

STEWART LITHGO
D.O.B. 2-6-57
Fights: 30 Wins: 16 Lost: 12 Drew: 2
Very tough. Stewie could take a lot of punishment and
was as game as a badger. Although he was too small for
a heavyweight, he still fought the best heavies in
Europe. He dropped down to cruiserweight and became
Commonwealth Champion.

BRIAN LONDON

Born 19-6-34

Fights: 58 Won: 37 Lost: 20 Drew: 1

Real name Brian Harper. Like his father Jack before him, Brian became British Heavyweight Champion. Always boxed out of Blackpool but was born and bred in Hartlepool. He had two cracks at the undisputed Heavyweight Championship of the World, losing to Floyd Patterson in 11 rounds in 1959 and Muhammad Ali in 3 rounds in 1966.

JACK LONDON

Born 21-6-13

Fights: 141 Won: 95 Lost: 39 Drew: 5 No Contests: 2

Real name John Harper. Big Jack received the princely sum of 12?p for his pro debut in 1931. He won the British Heavyweight title in 1944 and returned to Hartlepool a hero, with huge crowds waiting for him at the railway station. Jack had an astonishing 141 pro fights. Died in 1963 aged fifty.

BATTLING MANNERS

D.O.B. 1909

Fights: 19 Won: 11 Lost: 8

Real name George Manning. He sang in the church choir as a youngster and always had a good singing voice. Could often be heard belting a song or two out in the local pubs and clubs. He was also Hartlepool's first ever bouncer. He was a pro heavyweight in the 1930s and known locally as 'The Battler'. A crowd pleaser who had some fights at the Redworth Street 'Blood Tub'. A big man with hands like shovels and a cracking street fighter. Many stories have been told about The Battler, including when he knocked out four policemen. He died in December 1967 aged 58.

KEVIN MCKENZIE
D.O.B. 18-10-68
Welterweight
Fights: 25 Won: 9 Lost: 14 Drew: 2

Kev got cut non stop which was his downfall. His skin would tear open all the time. Northern Area Champ in '95 and retired in '96.

TONY ROWBOTHAM.
D.O.B. 24-1-72
Super Middleweight
Fights: 5 Won: 3 Lost: 2

I used to spar with Tony back in the 80's. He beat Mark Smith in the A.B.A Championships (Smith was tipped to win the title) but never fulfilled expectations. The Italian Stallion works as a builder.

MARK SMITH
Mark never turned pro but in the early 90's won the N.A.B.C (very prestigious national boxing competition) Championships 3 years in a row.

ALAN TEMPLE
Born 21-10-72
Fights: 30 Won: 13 Lost: 17
Alan was an excellent amateur who was double ABA
Champ and an England International who never fulfilled
his potential as a pro.

JAMES ROONEY
Born 30-4-78
Fights: 12 Won: 10 Lost: 2
James won every National title available as a junior, over
ten in total. Always had a large following that called
themselves the 'Roon Army'. The ABA title evaded him
but he reached the semi-finals in 1999. A gifted stand-up
boxer with excellent skills and a good boxing brain. He
turned pro and won 12 off the belt. Lost his last two and
retired. He says he has no intention of ever returning.

ANDREW TUCKER
D.O.B. 18-6-70
Middleweight
Fights: 2 Won: 1 Lost: 1
Andy captained Young England against Young USA and
won. Got to the quarter final of the Europeans and met
Gary Delaney in the Junior ABA Final and again in the
N.A.B.C Final, both winning one each.

ISAAC WARD

D.O.B. 7-4-77

Super Featherweight

Fights: 12 Won: 10 Lost: 0 Drew: 2

'Argy' will be looking to fight for a title of some kind soon. He reached the A.B.A Final as an amateur so the talent is there. Argy is of gypsy stock.

GARY WILKINSON

I fought Gary a couple of times in the early eighties. He was in his mid-twenties, very strong and powerful. Our fights were brutal affairs and we pushed our hearts and chins to the limit.

NIGEL WRIGHT

D.O.B. 22-6-79

Light Welterweight

Fights: 14 Won: 13 Lost: 1

Southpaw Nigel had a great amateur pedigree. Double A.B.A champion at Light Welterweight. England International. Multi Nations Silver Medal. Boxed in Commonwealth Games and World Championships. Is trained in Hartlepool by Peter Cope. Just won English Title with a 7th round KO.

EPILOGUE

When I think about it, I've been very lucky in my life. I have only been sent down to prison for three months. I know I've done a lot of damage to people in the past, which is all down to the way I hit. As the medium used to say, its a miracle I haven't killed anybody. I've had around one hundred street fights with only one loss, and that was when I was embarrassingly drunk. I have never looked for fights, but trouble has often looked for me. I have knocked out practically everybody in the metaphorical hard man's book of *Who's Who*.

But I'm going down a different path now. I have been a law-abiding citizen for a number of years. Yet I had to make a record of my past life, and so I decided to write this book. The opportunity presented itself while I was resting after the hernia operation. I admit I've had tears in my eyes and a few lumps in my throat recalling some of the stories. It has certainly stirred up the old memories. If you want to read more about my life, then there are four other books that feature me: *Viv Graham – The Final Chapter Volume 3* by Steve Richards; *Streetfighters* by Julian Davies; *What Makes Tough Guys* (6th Edition) by Jamie O'Keef; and *Bouncers* by Julian Davies and Terry Currie. You may well see me on TV soon, so don't worry if you missed my performance on *Surprise, Surprise*, as some media people have expressed an interest in doing a documentary about me. And there is a proposed film in the pipeline about the late Newcastle hard man Viv Graham, in which I have been promised a part.

As I write, I can also tell you that I have been offered a part in a film about Lenny McLean called *The Guv'nor*. I'm to play the part of an American heavyweight boxer who fights Roy Shaw, which will mean more painful training, but then again, I'm a glutton for punishment. Roy Shaw was Lenny McLean's archrival. I'm glad I am playing an American fighter, as all the best fighters seem to hail from that side of the pond. It is a place I have always wanted to visit. When filming starts, I'll just take each day one at a time and see how things go, since that is the Richy Horsley way.

Since the first edition of this book was published, I have turned my life around and now live the life of a peaceful warrior. I am a qualified Reiki healer and am also developing my skills as a trance medium.

Finally, I would like to thank my late mam, who passed away in 2005, just as the first edition of this book was reaching its final stages. Without my dear mother's help, I would never have been able to fully recollect some of the stories concerning my youth. But more importantly, without my dear mother's help, I might not have been around to recount any of it. Thanks, Mam.

Other titles by Stephen Richards available from John Blake Publishing

Insanity, My Mad Life
Charles Bronson with Stephen Richards
ISBN: 978-1-84454-030-3

The Krays and Me
Charles Bronson with Stephen Richards
ISBN: 978-1-84454-325-0

The Good Prison Guide
Charles Bronson with Stephen Richards
ISBN: 978-1-84454-359-5

The Lost Girl
Caroline Roberts with Stephen Richards
ISBN: 978-1-84358-148-2

It's Criminal
James Crosbie with Stephen Richards
ISBN: 978-1-84454-059-4

Street Warrior
Malcolm Price with Stephen Richards
ISBN: 978-1-84454-299-4

Crash 'n' Carry
Stephen Richards
ISBN: 978-1-84454-106-5

The Tax Man
Brian Cockerill with Stephen Richards
ISBN: 978-1-84454-488-2

Lost in Care
Jimmy Holland with Stephen Richards
ISBN: 978-1-84454-361-8

Viv Graham
Stephen Richards
ISBN: 978-1-84454-127-0

Scottish Hard Bastards
Jimmy Holland with Stephen Richards
978-1-84454-459-2

Fight to the Death
Stephen Richards
978-1-84454-245-1

Psycho Steve
Steve Moyle with Stephen Richards
978-1-84454-251-2

Solitary Fitness
Charles Bronson with Stephen Richards
978-1-84454-251-2

Heart of Darkness
Lynette Gould with Stephen Richards
978-1-84454-605-3